Frank M

A Bit of Good Luck

To Joselyn & Mike

Best wishes
And enjoy the reads!

Austin Macauley Publishers™

LONDON · CAMBRIDGE · NEW YORK · SHARJAH

Frank McGurk is retired and lives in Donegal with his wife, Audrey. During the recent lockdown, he took to writing about some of his memories from his early years. In this book, he shares some of those memories with you.

For
Leo, Naomi, Penelope and Hugo.

A CIP catalogue record for this title is available from the British Library.

ISBN 9781398424678 (Paperback)
ISBN 9781398424685 (ePub e-book)

www.austinmacauley.com

First Published 2023
Austin Macauley Publishers Ltd®
1 Canada Square
Canary Wharf
London
E14 5AA

I would like to thank all my family; my wife, Audrey, my son and daughter-in-law, Leo and Cheryl and my daughter and son-in-law, Emma and Bob.

They all encouraged me to keep writing, when there were times when I had second thoughts.

But then I thought of those words spoken at that famous dinner party.

"To make each day count" And so that's what I've done, I've tried to make each day count.

Proudly supporting
The Parkinson's Association of Ireland.

Table of Contents

1
A Bit of Good Luck

A young lad heads off on a hitch-hiking journey…
Does he realise what he's letting himself in for?

It was a bright crisp morning with barely a cloud in the sky, but you would not go without a coat as there was just the slightest hint of autumn in the air. The few remaining stars that could still be seen were battling hard against the rising sun, and soon they were gone too.

It was early in August 1969 and the swinging sixties were just coming to an end.

That August saw the real beginning of the Troubles in Northern Ireland. Worldwide, the war in Vietnam was still raging and the United States had put a man on the moon – actually two men, and brought them safely back to earth – as predicted by President Kennedy in 1961. It was the year of Woodstock and the Manson murders. Richard Nixon was sworn in as 37th President of America and, just a few days after this story, The Beatles would be photographed walking across the pedestrian crossing on Abbey Road.

But none of this bothered me in the least as I walked out the front gate of our house near Carrigans in County Donegal and, glancing back, saw my mother standing at the kitchen window, waving goodbye to me with her walking stick. I waved back. It was about 5.30 a.m. and there wasn't a sound in the air.

My father had secured a railway-lifting contract in Fermoy in County Cork at that time. Railway lines and branch lines were closing all over Ireland between 1960 and 1972 and my father had carried out most of the lifting contracts around the country for the previous ten years or so. He had left home on Monday morning to go to Fermoy and, as I was on school holiday, I was to go with him. As it was the end of the salmon net-fishing season which we were involved in on the River Foyle, we had two men organised for that same Monday morning to wash the nets, before hanging up to dry for the winter. But one of the men hadn't turned up, so I had to deputise and it was going to take all day. My father couldn't delay his journey, so he went on and I said I would get up early on Tuesday and hitch-hike it to Fermoy.

It brings a shudder to me now, as a father and a grandfather, when I think of a lad of seventeen heading off on his own to hitch-hike from Donegal to Cork. From County Donegal, in the very northernmost peninsula of the country, to County Cork, way down in the south. Nowadays all this just wouldn't happen for a number of reasons: one, no-one would lift a stranger in these times; two, no-one would get into a car with a stranger or strangers; three, most main roads have been replaced with motorways and you can't walk or stop on a motorway; and four, for insurance reasons, no-one would lift you anyway. Hitch-hikers are almost an extinct species. But hitch-hiking or 'thumbing' a lift was very popular in the fifties, right through to the seventies. So to hitch-hike it from Donegal to Cork was really no big deal, in those days. Many people, the young and the not so young, hitch-hiked.

So, that morning, as the day was dawning, I left the house with my duffel bag on my back, my body amply fortified with Mammy's breakfast, my soul with a liberal sprinkling of her holy water, and in my pocket a pound note, enough for a couple of meals along the way.

So began the long trek to Fermoy. Of course I hoped, as every hitch-hiker did in those days, that there wouldn't be too much actual walking and that lifts would be plentiful and without much delay between them. I had hitch-hiked before and I always had a plan which, generally speaking, worked for me.

My plan was simple: keep the footwork to a minimum.

I reckoned that if a driver is going to lift you, he's going to lift you anyway, so there's no point in walking further than necessary. That meant, for instance, I always picked a spot on the outside of a town or a road junction, where traffic had to slow anyway. And that was where the best chance of getting a lift was. If you walked for a mile out of any town, the drivers had increased their speed and it was less likely that they would stop for a hitch-hiker. I had always found that it was much harder to get a lift on the country road, than on the edge of a town. Once drivers had left town, they tended to be reluctant to stop on a main road. Especially when the traffic was heavy.

Most of my previous hitch-hiking was from Derry to our home across the border, although I had thumbed from our home to Magilligan near Limavady before. In Derry, at the edge of the city, there was a petrol filling station which had the advantage of being on the left side as you left the city. In those days if I stood at the exit from the filling station, I was nearly always fortunate that a car leaving town would stop for me. Especially if he or she had been in for a fill of petrol. In that case, it was almost a dead cert. He or she was practically stopped anyhow as they emerged on to the main road.

The methodology was always the same – catch their attention, raise your arm and extended thumb, put on a sad face, look them straight in the eye, and nine times out of ten you were home and dry.

Of course there were times that you thought the car was going to stop, but it slowed, took one look and drove on. I wouldn't be human if I didn't admit to throwing a few choice words after him or her, out of earshot of course. Perhaps wishing the driver bad luck, like getting a puncture and having no spare wheel. Not very Christian I know, but I'm sure Jesus himself, if he'd been thumbing home to Nazareth after a big night out, for instance, and somebody passed him by in a cart without as much as a glance, he wouldn't have been too pleased either! Mightn't he have wished that a spoke or two on the wheel of the said cart would snap in a Galilean pothole?

Probably.

Of course if it did break a couple of spokes, it's likely, given that we are told he was handy with the old carpentry tools, he would have got the job of fixing it anyway. Then, if he had any sense, he could have really got his own back and bogged the arm in!

There is one part of hitch-hiking that you simply cannot plan and that is your progress. It's really all down to luck. You can have a good day when every car at every stop lifts you and leaves you at your next destination, and then there are other days when you just hit a bad run. You just never know.

But anyway, that morning, as I walked away from our house, I was planning where my best spots were likely to be. The first part of my journey was from home to Raphoe, which I reckoned would be easy enough, and from Raphoe it should be handy enough to get to Ballybofey. From Ballybofey to Donegal Town should be okay too. The plan for the journey after Donegal Town was to find a good location, just outside the town, in order to catch the Sligo traffic. For that I reckoned the best spot was just past Floods Ford garage, where there was a sharp bend which was also the end of the thirty-miles-per-hour zone. A lift from here should take me all the way to Sligo, but to which side of Sligo was a factor to consider...It was a long walk through the town to get to the other side. So, I hoped my lift would drop me off closer to the far side of town from where, with any luck, another pick up would take me on to Galway. From Galway to Limerick could pose a problem as there was a bypass by Oranmore, which circumvented Galway City, and the traffic was usually heavy so drivers were reluctant to stop on this stretch of road, but I looked on the bright side – maybe I would get one lift from Sligo right through to Limerick. From Limerick to Mallow and from Mallow to Fermoy were unknown territories to me but I reckoned I'd cross those bridges when I got to them.

But first things first – let's get to Raphoe. I'd worry about the next stage then.

Now there was, and still is of course, a crossroads at the end of our minor road, about a hundred and fifty yards from our house, so I planned to make that my first port of departure and wait there for the first Good Samaritan who might be heading in the direction of Raphoe. If fortune was on my side and I managed to make thirty-five miles every hour, I should be in Fermoy around two or three o'clock in the afternoon. At the very worst, four o'clock. What helped was that it was a dry and sunny day, so people were more likely to lift you. No-one wanted a soaking wet hitch-hiker in their car.

I was studying all this in my mind, having clocked up about fifty or sixty yards, when I heard from behind me the unmistakeable sound of a van approaching. The road was narrow, so I stepped back onto the grass verge to let it pass. I looked at the driver and he looked at me and then, with a screech of his brakes, he slowed to a stop.

Could this be the first of a good run of lifts? I asked myself, as I ran to the passenger door. I pulled the handle, the door opened and before I had a chance to ask him where he was going, the driver said, "Where you headin' then, boyo?"

"Fermoy, in County Cork. But anywhere in that direction would do."

"Well, bejaysus," says he, "this is your lucky day, boyo, for I'm going to Cork too, so I am. Hop in."

I couldn't believe it – one lift the whole way!

What a bit of good luck, I said to myself as I jumped in. *I'll be there before I know it.*

I reached out for the door handle strap and he said, "Give it a good slam." So I gave it a good slam!

He crunched the gearstick into first and off we headed. The clutch had obviously seen a lot of miles, as he had trouble at times finding the right gear. It was one of those gear levers which was up on the steering column, and I knew enough about cars to know that when these began to wear with age they could give a lot of trouble.

The smell of smoke was awful in the van. Whether cigarette smoke or exhaust fumes, I wasn't sure. But as it turned out it was a combination of both. With, as I would soon find out, a frequent ejection of methane. Not to mention the smell of fish as well. Nothing was said by either of us until he got off the side road and on to the main road and put the gearstick through its motions, got a bit of speed up going down the first hill and eventually he managed to get her in to top gear. But his top gear got him to only about forty miles per hour – and that was on the level!

It was obvious that the old van had seen better days. In fact, it was almost clapped out. It was one of those early ones, where the engine was in the cab between the driver and the passenger, under a cover. It wasn't like the modern version of vans, where the passenger seat is a double seat. This van had a single seat for the driver, a similar one for the passenger, and the engine in between. The first problem was that there was a hole in the exhaust, which made talking virtually a shouting match and secondly, the hole was allowing fumes to escape and of course, they 'escaped' into the cab. I was soon thinking to myself, by the time I get to Cork, if one gas doesn't get me, the other will.

But anyway, I contented myself in the knowledge that it was better than no lift – beggars can't be choosers and all that.

Once he got her up to 'speed' he reached for a packet of Players cigarettes that was lying on the dash, pushed open the box exposing the cigarettes, and offered me one. I thanked him but declined. He took one out for himself, closed the packet and, as men used to do with unfiltered cigarettes, he tapped it a couple or three times on the box – first one end, then the other – and put it into his mouth. He produced a box of matches from his coat pocket, struck one, and more from force of habit, obviously, than protection from the nonexistent breeze, cupped his hands around the flame and lit the cigarette. Having shaken the match to extinction, he wound down the window a fraction and threw it out. I wondered why he bothered as the inside of the van hadn't seen cleaning since the day it left the showroom. But it was either throw it on the floor or throw it out the window. The option of the ashtray was a definite non-starter, as it was full to the brim with cigarette ends and didn't look as though it had been emptied in ages. He wound up the window again, and then took an enormous draw from the cigarette. This instigated a splutter of coughing, which lasted the best part of half a minute, after which he screwed down his window again and parted with a mouthful of spittle. Then, after giving his mouth a rub with his sleeve, said, "Ah, Jaysus, that's better."

To this day, how inhaling a load of smoke into one's lungs would make a person feel better, beats me, but sure, as they say, it takes all kinds.

When he got himself all settled, he turned and said, "I'm Jimmy, by the way," holding out his hand, complete with sweat and nicotine-stained fingers and God knows what else. But I shook it anyway and said, "I'm Frank."

I'm sure I thought at the time he was an old man but looking back now I would put him at about forty-five, maybe fifty years old. Isn't it funny how you look at a person's age, when you're only seventeen? Everyone over thirty is old and those around sixty – well, they're ancient, aren't they?

It wasn't long before the obvious question came.

"So where are you from, Frankie?"

I didn't correct his calling me Frankie. I didn't really mind anyway. I told him I lived just about a mile back, in fact just up the road from where he lifted me.

He then asked me what took me to Fermoy at that time of the morning on my own. I explained to him that my father was in the railway salvaging business and that, at that time, he was lifting the stretch from Mallow to Fermoy.

"Oh is he, now?" he said. "He'll be a busy man then, the way things are going."

"Yes," I said. "Next year I think he is going to lift a line somewhere in Tipperary."

"Arragh," he said. "That'll be the line from Clonmel up to Horse and Jockey. Sure they closed it down last year. But I suppose it was doing nothing, anyway."

He paused and took a long draw from his cigarette.

"I'll tell you now Frankie, in twenty years, there'll not be a train left in Ireland the way they're going, not a train left," he said, with a melancholy shake of his head.

After a moment's silence, I countered his curiosity.

"So what takes you up to this part of the world, at this time of the morning?"

"I left Greencastle this morning at three o'clock," he said, "I'm in the fish business and every couple of weeks or so I'm in different parts of the country, but I only come up here the odd time."

His accent told me that he was from somewhere way down south, but I couldn't pin it down to anywhere in particular. As far as I was concerned, he had a 'southern' accent and that was that. Although, when he spoke, he did remind me of the guy who we would often hear on the radio commentating on all the big Gaelic football matches. But, to me, all southern Irish accents sounded the same.

"I drive for a fish firm in Cork, but I also buy and sell a bit of stuff myself. That's where I'm heading with this load," he said, nodding to the rear of the van. I assumed there was a mixture of fish in the back. It certainly smelled like a mixture of fish, anyway.

"I was down at the river, talking to some of the salmon boys, before I lifted you, but they hadn't caught much last night," he said.

"I know some of the fishermen down there," I said.

"Do ye?" he said, with a look of surprise. "And who do you know?"

"I know the Browns and the Harkins and the Tolands."

"Ah, Jaysus, sure you know more of them than I do. Sure I buy an odd box of salmon from them, from time to time," he said. "Grand lads, those boys, aye, grand lads."

"Ah, do you?" I said, and the conversation died for a moment.

He then began singing a song, which I was unfamiliar with, but which I certainly knew the name of before the day was out. It was called 'Mother Machree', but all he seemed to know was the first and last lines of the chorus.

"Sure I love the dear silver that shines in your hair…"

Then he would hum or *"da da da"* the middle bit, which he obviously didn't know the words of, and then burst into the last line.

"Ohhhhhh…God bless you and keep you, Mother Machree."

If I heard 'Mother Machree' once that day, I must have heard it a hundred times. By evening, if I had got hold of Mother Machree, I would have throttled the old bastard.

There were no seat belts, of course. Jimmy didn't sit upright with his hands on the wheel, but more or less lay on top of it with his arms folded across it. Not the safest of a posture, but I suppose at the speed he was driving, it hardly made much difference. Needless to say, there was no radio either.

There wasn't much power in the old van, but there was little traffic on the road and so, although he didn't drive too fast, we were soon through Raphoe and Convoy and heading for Ballybofey. We were making reasonably good time, I thought. There was hardly a person out and about in the towns and villages at that early hour, so it was a clear run through Ballybofey and on to the long haul up towards Barnesmore Gap. As we climbed McGrory's Brae, he dropped her a couple of gears which, of course, made the fumes and the noise worse. I reached for the winder to screw down the window a bit, before I was gassed completely, but the handle just turned without the window moving. So much for that plan. But there was a little quarter window which I managed to push open, and that helped a little.

As we levelled out just before the Gap, alongside Lough Mourne, I asked him to stop a minute saying that I needed a pee. But what I really wanted was a breath of fresh air. I was nearly blue in the face from the carbon monoxide.

After a few minutes by the roadside, I was okay again and about to get into the van, when he got out and walked round to the back of the van and said, "C'mere a minute, Frankie."

He proceeded to open the double doors and, to my amazement, a sight appeared to me the like of which I had never seen before, nor have I since.

Stacked to the roof were crates upon crates, and in the crates were lobsters. At least he told me they were lobsters – I suspect they were big crabs. I couldn't see in properly, but they were all making a cacophony of noise. Now whether it was from their vocal cords, which I doubt as I don't know whether crustaceans have vocal cords or not but I suspect they don't, or from their claws, or their tails all rubbing together, I'll never know. But it sounded like a thousand sheets of sandpaper, all rubbing against each other.

Now behind one of the back doors and standing beside the spare wheel was a five-gallon drum and a bucket. Jimmy reached in and pulled out the drum, which was full of clean water. He unscrewed the lid and poured half of the contents into the bucket, almost filling it. The left-hand side rear door he was able to keep open by itself, by way of a spring clasp, but the right-side clasp was broken, so he said, "Frankie, can you hold that door open for me?"

So I held the door open as wide as I could, and, taking the bucket of water, he stood back, took a short run up to the van and threw the water over the crabs, or lobsters, or whatever they were.

"Keeps 'em moist," he said.

Aye and kept me moist too, I said to myself, as most of the water bounced back off the crates and splashed over me. How much water actually got into the crates would be anyone's guess. He got a splash over himself too, but he didn't seem to mind.

He repeated the operation, emptying the remaining water from the drum into the bucket.

This time I was more aware, and I stood more behind the door, but still got some over me.

"That'll keep them right for a while," he said, screwing the cap back on the now empty drum, placing it and the bucket inside, jamming them with one door and then closing the second door to keep the whole lot secure.

"Now, remind me to fill the water jar again at our next stop, Frankie," he said. What I called a 'drum', he called a 'jar'.

"Okay," I said, wondering how he managed other times without me. I jumped into the passenger seat, and slammed the door as previously instructed, but no sign of him appeared. I glanced at the outside mirror and in the reflection I could see him, standing having a piss against the side of the van. He finished with a shake of his leg, gave the rear tyre a kick, walked around the back of the van and in he climbed.

As he stepped up, he let out a long odious fart and quickly said, "Oh, oh…better out, Frankie, better out. Arragh, it's the tablets, you know, it's the tablets."

I never did know whether he meant better out of him or better out of the van!

As far as I was concerned, better out of both!

He screwed down his window, parted company with another spittle, wound the window back up and then reached for his cigarettes. When he struck the match, he automatically brought his knee up to the steering wheel to leave his both hands free. I feared that this was a harbinger of what was ahead of me.

I'm not sure which gas was worse, the carbon monoxide from the engine or the methane from Jimmy's farts.

Twenty minutes later and we were in the Diamond in Donegal Town. But instead of heading left out towards Sligo, he turns right and says that he had to do a short detour to Killybegs – something about having to see a man about fish!

"Won't be five minutes," he added. So we trundled out through Mountcharles, Dunkineely and Bruckless and eventually we reached Killybegs. This detour was going to hold us back a bit, *but hopefully not too long*, I thought to myself. He pulled the van to a stop outside a pub, up a bit from the harbour.

It was still only about seven o'clock and, after a moment, he turned the key and the engine died. The silence was deafening but very welcome, although I could still hear the strange chorus in the back. Nothing was astir except the seagulls and the distant *thump-thump* of a Kelvin engine.

The pub was – naturally, given the early hour – still closed. Jimmy just sat there, lit another cigarette and muttered, after the fit of coughing subsided, "He'll be out in a minute."

Sure enough, after about two minutes, the door was opened a fraction and a man beckoned us inside.

"Close your door gently," Jimmy said to me – an action, which was a pointless exercise, as far as that van was concerned. As soon as we entered the premises, the man quietly closed the door behind us and we went towards the bar. Jimmy took a stool and pulled himself up on to it. I did likewise.

"The usual, Jimmy?" says the man. Jimmy nodded and then the man looks over at me.

"Who's the lad with you today?" He was looking back at Jimmy, rather than asking me.

"He's hitch-hiking his way to Cork and I lifted him a few miles back."

"What will you have, lad? A mineral?"

I didn't think he would have Football Special, a locally made cola that I was fond of, but then I saw he had a row of them on the bottom shelf.

"Aye, okay. I'll have a Football Special, thanks." I was a bit surprised at the emergence of drink on the counter at that hour of the morning, but I held my tongue, naturally.

The man turned and pushed a small glass up to the spirits optic, allowing a half-measure of Bushmills whiskey to pour in. I noticed that his trousers' braces were all twisted at the back – obviously he got out of bed in a hurry and didn't put them on straight. He reached for a bottle of Guinness and a bottle of Football Special and pulled the tops off them. He set them on the bar along with two glasses, but he made no attempt to pour them. I mumbled another "thank you" to no-one in particular, as I didn't know who was buying. All I was sure of was that it certainly wasn't me!

Jimmy poured his own drink and I followed suit. In the days before draught Guinness, it was all bottles and many men preferred to pour their own. The head had to be just right, so after pouring the glass was normally set on the counter for a few seconds until the head settled.

All I could think about was perhaps being stuck here for a couple of hours. But Jimmy downed half the Guinness in the first mouthful and then he followed up with the whiskey in a strange way – a strange way to me, anyway. He drank half of the whiskey and poured the remainder into the glass of Guinness.

He let out a belch, excused himself, and then said to the barman, "Much happening, Sean Óg?"

"No, very little this week," says Sean Óg. "Paddy Bán was the best of them and he only got about twenty. I think that's going to be it for this year, Jimmy, unless there's a few at the back end."

"I doubt it now," says Jimmy, "Bit far on in the year... Anyway, here you go and sure we'll have another deal again."

As he said this, he handed the barman an envelope which obviously contained some money. "There's the few pounds I owed you from the last time, Sean Óg, and thanks again. Anyway, we must push on. What do I owe you for the drink?" Jimmy pulled a handful of coins from his trouser pocket.

"Ah, forget it, Jimmy," says Sean Óg, "Sure I'll get you again. Tell me, if there is a few more fish before it's over, would you be interested?"

"Always interested, Sean, always in the market. Give me a call anytime," says Jimmy.

With that, he put the money back in his pocket, downed the rest of the Guinness, got up and gave his mouth a wipe with his coat sleeve. He turned to go and I followed him, but before Sean Óg opened the door, I said to Jimmy, "What about the water drum?"

"What drum?" he asked, before it dawned on him that I meant what he called the jar.

"Oh, Bejaysus, you're right, Frankie, the water jar. Would you scoot out and bring it in? Good lad."

Sean Óg let me out and I went to the van and brought in the drum. Sean Óg took it somewhere out the back and filled it to the brim.

"He does well here," whispered Jimmy, while Sean Óg was out. *"Always busy."*

Eventually he returned and carried it right through and left it at the back of the van. Jimmy opened the back door, set it in and closed it again, as quietly as he could. As Sean Óg walked away, I said, "Thanks for the mineral."

Without turning, he gave a slight wave and said something which I didn't catch. Whatever it was, I think it was in Irish.

We both climbed in and closed the doors as gently as we could.

"That's it, Frankie Boy, let's go," says he and turned on the ignition and pulled the starter. After few turns, the engine fired and a puff of smoke blew into the cab.

"He's a decent boyo, is Sean Óg," said Jimmy, as he turned on to the main street. "I know him a long time and if he says he has good fish, he has good fish. Never let me down, aye, a decent boyo." He reached for his cigarettes.

"Sure I love the dear silver that shines in your hair...,
Da da da da da da da da da da da da..."

And off we headed.

Back through those same little villages which were just then beginning to stir. *If they haven't stirred by now,* I thought, *they certainly will with the noise of this yoke driving through.* In what seemed like no time, we were in Donegal Town again and turning left he drove out of the Diamond. A signpost across the road, pointing left, said 'SLIGO'. We were back on track (or so I thought!). Hopefully, we would soon make up the lost time. And I had enjoyed the Football Special.

So on we went, through Ballintra and Laghey and in to Ballyshannon. As we drove over the bridge in Ballyshannon, he said, nodding past me, "See that big dam up there, that's a big electricity power station. Powers half the country, it does, powers half the country."

"Is that right?"

I was about to say, "I know that. I've done this journey before on a few occasions and my father told me all about these things and places," but then I thought, *I'll just say nothing.*

And while the humming in the back remained constant – in fact I got used to it and hardly heard it, especially with the engine running – the humming in the front would rise until…

"Ohhhhhhh…God bless you and keep you, Mother Machree."

Between Ballyshannon and Bundoran, he pulled into the side of the road, pulled the handbrake, which I think was a waste of time, and said, "Come on Frankie, more water."

And the routine was conducted again. The back doors were opened, the two buckets of water thrown over the crabs – and some over us. "Keeps 'em moist," he muttered. Again. Bucket and drum set inside, doors slammed shut. Then he took a leak behind the van, gave the tyre a kick, climbed back inside, lit a cigarette, followed by a bout of coughing and finishing with a spit out the window. Although I heard no resonance, I was sure I detected a waft of methane.

A turn of the key, a pull of the starter and off we went. Again. The whole episode didn't take too long, so that was okay.

"Sure I love the dear silver that shines in your hair…"

"Have you a puncture?" I asked, having seen him kick the tyre a couple of times.

"Arragh, I think I've a slow one," he said, "but sure I haven't a minute to get it fixed."

On through Bundoran and shops were beginning to open, a couple of awnings already down. I was keeping an eye out for any girls, but I didn't see any. Probably still in their beds. There were a few women out walking, but they were 'oul biddies', about twenty-five or thirty years old, at least. Sure when you're only seventeen, as I have said, aren't all women over nineteen or twenty, 'oul biddies'? Then we were on that long stretch to Sligo. But suddenly, he glanced at his watch and said, "Oh, I almost forgot, Frankie, I need to do a quick stop in Mullaghmore."

My immediate reaction was to say, *Fuck sake, not again, Jimmy,* but I held my tongue, as they say. About half a mile further on, at the junction into Mullaghmore, he took a right turn. The village wasn't too far off the beaten track, only about a mile from the main road, so I hoped it wouldn't be a long stop. As we got close to the village, the castle loomed large and bright in the morning sunshine.

"See that big castle?" said Jimmy.

Well, I did know who owned it and who lived there and I knew what Jimmy was going to say, but I just said "Aye."

"Y'know, a big British Lord lives there in the summer, Lord…Lord…Mac somebody or other. He's related to the Queen, ye know. And he comes here on holiday every year. Ah, Jaysus, his name will come to me in a minute!" he says, as he scratched his head.

I knew it was Lord Mountbatten, but I didn't say, just to see if he would remember. But he didn't.

After three or four minutes, we reached the village and, sure enough, just as I expected, he pulled in at another hostelry off the main street and out we got. Jimmy took the empty water drum out of the van.

This establishment wasn't open yet either, but a quick knock and soon a curtain was drawn back a little in a bay window and a woman peeped out. On recognising Jimmy, she shook her head to the left, indicating we were to go around to the side entrance. So we walked round the corner and, just as we reached it, she unbarred the door, opened it back a little, stuck her head out, and took a quick glance up and down the street. She then opened the door just enough to allow us past. She had a freshly lit cigarette hanging from her lips. While we were there, she never seemed to remove it, but just smoked away with it in her mouth.

"You can't be too careful. There's always a few extra Guards about, when himself's here," she said, with her thumb pointing away behind her, in the direction of the castle. So in we go, Jimmy carrying the empty water drum. She proceeded down a hallway and as she passed the stairs, she stopped and looked up.

"PAAAAT, Jimmy's here," she half roared, yet half whispered, if you know what I mean.

"Righto," a man's voice answered, from somewhere above.

Then it was in through a door to the left, which opened into the lounge part. Jimmy and I followed her.

Again, the place was empty and, in fact, last night's glasses and bottles still littered the tables. The windows had curtains pulled and this made the place somewhat dark. And the place smelled.

A moment or two later, Pat came down and spotting Jimmy, he says, "How's Jimmy? You're early on the go." He nodded in my direction. "Have you a young helper with you today?"

"Ah, no," says Jimmy. "He's a gossun* from up in Donegal and he's hitching a lift to Fermoy and he was lucky that I came along and sure I'll be able to leave him the whole way there."

"Ah, right, I see" says Pat. "And what part of Donegal?" He lifted a dirty cloth and gave the counter a cursory rub. He didn't make eye contact with me.

"Near a wee village called Carrigans," I said.

"Ahhhh," was all he said.

"Near Derry," I added, but he didn't hear me, he wasn't listening. He obviously hadn't a clue where Carrigans was. He ignored me and turned to Jimmy. I didn't like the man. Why, I don't know. I just remember that I didn't like him.

"Stout, Jimmy?"

Although, technically, a 'stout' could mean a number of different beers, in most of Ireland, it almost exclusively means a bottle of Guinness.

Jimmy said, "Okay." Then, dropping his voice, "I'll just visit the wee room first."

He headed out the back and as I had taken a dislike to Pat. I didn't want to be with him on my own, so I followed Jimmy, deciding also that it might be a while before the next stop. When he opened the door, I was nearly felled. There are no words to describe the stink of those toilets. I remember it to

---

* **Gossun**, *from Irish, 'gasur', French/Norman, 'garcon', a boy, a lad.*

this very day. They say you never forget a smell – it stays with you. And this is a true fact, for if ever I go into a smelly toilet, it reminds me of that one in Mullaghmore. If there was a league for stinking toilets, this one was up there in the Premiership.

It was awful. I'd heard of but never seen the Black Hole of Calcutta, but my betting was that it was no worse than what I had just visited.

I stood there beside Jimmy and pulled down my zip, while he struggled with buttons and both of us began taking a pee. The actual urinal consisted of one large stainless-steel sheet, screwed to the wall, with the outlet pipe at one end plumbed out through the wall to God knows where – probably to the back yard! The end of the urinal was blocked with cigarette ends and the piss lying in its gutter was about two inches deep.

Nothing was said between us, so for a bit of fun, I said to Jimmy with a straight face, "I wonder, Jimmy, if Lord Mountbatten was in here last night?"

This set Jimmy off on a fit of laughing and he laughed so much that he started a bout of coughing, which made him bend over with the result that he missed the urinal completely and pissed all over his shoes – and then to top it all off, he let go a chain of farts.

"Oops," was all he could say between the laughing and the coughing, which then started me off laughing, as well. If it wasn't for the sound, you would never have noticed his farts, lost in the myriad of smells in that hellhole.

There was one dirty sink and cold water tap, but no drying towels of any sort, so it was a quick rinse and a shake of our hands in the air, after which I finished with a rub on my trousers and, after waiting a few moments in an effort to stifle the laughter and Jimmy's coughing, we went back out to the bar, keeping faces as straight as we could. But Pat just says, "There's your jar refilled again, Jimmy," with a nod towards the drum of water, now standing beside the door.

I couldn't wait to get out of there. Apart from the smell, there was just something I didn't like about the place.

A bottle of Guinness and a half of whiskey stood on the bar in front of Jimmy.

"Would you like anything, sonny?" Pat asked.

I told him I was fine. Even if I'd wanted one, I couldn't stomach the thought of it after coming out of those 'toilets'.

And I didn't like being called "sonny".

Jimmy proffered a ten-shilling note to Pat, but Pat said, "Ah no Jimmy, sure anyway the till drawer is upstairs."

After a large swig of Guinness, leaving him a froth moustache, Jimmy says, "Anything happening, Pat, is there much about?" By that I assumed that he meant salmon.

"No, very poor here all week. What about above in Greencastle?" asked Pat.

"Much the same. Ah, sure if there's none here, there'll be none in Greencastle."

"No, I suppose not."

After a bit of small talk, Jimmy drank half the whiskey, fortified the rest of the Guinness with the remainder and then downed the lot. His coat sleeve did the necessary to his lips. From the look of it, it would be hard to put a number on how many microbes thrived in that coat sleeve!

"Right, Frankie, we'll hit the trail."

"Aye, right," I said, in total agreement as I made my way towards the door.

"If there are any fish in the late run, Pat, sure you can gimme a bell."

"I certainly will, I certainly will," said Pat. "Good luck to ye now."

Before he opened the door, his wife, complete with a fresh cigarette hanging from her lips, looked out through the bay window, up the street and down the street.

"All clear, go on, go on," she whispered, matching her words with a wave of her arm.

What the point of whispering was, I couldn't figure out. But I suppose it was all part of the game between pubs and the authorities.

Jimmy set the drum of water in the back of the van and in we got – again. The routine was identical: a turn of the key, pull of the starter knob, a hesitant start, a cigarette, a bout of coughing, the dispatch of another spittle, his battle with the gearstick to find first gear, and away we went. And despite the smell in the van, it was a thousand times better than the smell from where we just left.

"Sure I love the dear silver, that shines in your hair…"

Then, suddenly he stopped singing and straightened up.

"Didn't I tell you there's a big important Englishman lives up there in that big castle, in the summertime. Lord Mac something…" he said, pointing to the castle.

Jesus, here we go again, I thought, before I decided to tell him.

"Lord Mountbatten," I said. "And he's a cousin of the Queen."

Jimmy slapped his thigh.

"Arragh, bejaysus, Frankie, you're right, that's his name. Lord Mountbatten, that's it. Sure I knew it would come to me."

He had obviously forgotten that I had mentioned Lord Mountbatten while we were in the toilet, ten minutes ago. "And sure he's a cousin or something of the Queen, did ye know?"

"Is he?"

I had come to the conclusion that it would be better to just agree. I feared his memory was like the clutch – slipping a bit. Or more likely the drink had something to do with it!

As he slowed up at a junction with the main road, Jimmy pulled her back into second gear, glanced to his right and said, "Are we okay your side, Frankie?" putting down the boot and driving on out, without stopping.

I never got time to speak, but luckily there were no vehicles coming. If there had been, it was curtains for them, or us, or both. When he got her into top gear, I tried to get as comfortable as I could for the long road ahead. I pushed my duffel bag and coat into the corner behind me and attempted to lie back against it. We were a good bit behind my hoped-for schedule. *But what the hell*, I thought, *sure we're back on the road now.*

"Ohhhhhh, God bless you and keep you, Mother Machree."

At this stage it was about eleven thirty or so, and I could see that Jimmy was none the better from the two stouts and two whiskeys. He was a bit tipsy.

And I was getting tired.

But we soldiered on and travelled down past the towering cliffs of Ben Bulben and into Yeats Country, Drumcliffe, and we soon passed the little church graveyard where the famous bard lies. I was about to ask Jimmy if he knew who was buried in there, but then I thought, *No, I'll not bother. If he knows, he knows and if he doesn't, he doesn't.* As we drove past, I glanced in over the little cemetery wall and managed a quick look at the grave. A couple of tourists were standing at the graveside, reading the inscription. I had been at Yeats' grave before with my father and I knew the wording of the epitaph well enough.

CAST A COLD EYE
ON LIFE, ON DEATH.
HORSEMAN, PASS BY.

And that's exactly what we did. We passed by.

Soon we hit Sligo and managed to get through the town without too much trouble, and Jimmy made only one stop there and that was for petrol.

On we went, through Ballysadare and past the big Volkswagen garage, under the railway bridge tunnel and on to Collooney, then taking a right for Tobercurry and Charlestown. Of course, nowadays, the garage, the tunnel and indeed Ballysadare itself have all been bypassed with motorway.

Halfway up the street in Charlestown, we crossed the boundary from County Sligo into County Mayo. Not that you would notice – Mayo potholes are much the same as Sligo potholes. In the Market Square, Jimmy takes a right turn out of town instead of a left and, anticipating my question, he says, "Are you okay, if we go out to Westport to see a man? He owes me a few bob."

"Aye, of course," I said as if my opinion mattered. I reckoned he thought I wouldn't notice the latest detour. But I was in Charlestown before and, even without the signposts, I knew that this wasn't the direct road to Galway. We were going west, instead of south.

How many more detours? I wondered.

On through Swinford and then Castlebar and finally we reached Westport. Beautiful countryside and scenery, no doubt. But not when viewed from the inside of a clapped out, noisy, smelly old van.

At this stage it was about one o'clock or maybe a bit more and I was really hungry. It seemed so long ago, now, since I finished off that bowl of Mammy's porridge.

The only stop we made since leaving Sligo was outside Swinford, at a wee pub and petrol pumps along the side of the road. We went through the same routine: a splash, a slash, another half and a bottle and a mineral "for the boyo". I don't think the barman knew Jimmy that well, as all he said was, "Howya Sir, long time no see."

Jimmy just replied that he hadn't been this way in a while. Very little more was said, and he took the money from Jimmy and left the change on the counter. He didn't engage Jimmy in any chat; he was more interested in the horse-racing pages of the *Irish Independent*, which he had spread out on the counter, and a bag of crisps that he was going through as if it was the last bag in Ireland. Occasionally, he muttered to himself and ticked off, with the stub of a pencil, what was obviously a horse he fancied in a particular race. After about ten minutes, we got up to go and Jimmy asked if he could get the water jar filled. The barman just nodded, gave a grunt through a mouthful of crisps and pointed in the general direction of the door, indicating that there was a tap outside. Jimmy lifted his change off the counter, we said our goodbyes and left. Sure enough, there was a tap beside the pumps.

"He's a bundle of fun," I said to Jimmy, as we began to fill the drum.

"Ah sure what do you expect from a Blueshirt[*]?" he replied.

I didn't understand what he meant at the time.

I told Jimmy I would lift the water drum into the van. He grunted something and nodded his head as he walked, or more precisely staggered, round to his side of the van. I screwed the lid back on the drum, set it in the back of the van beside the bucket, shut the doors, jumped in, and on we went.

Jimmy, at this stage, was really in no fit state to drive, so what he did was drop the speed. Another cigarette was lit, the empty box fired out of the window and Jimmy lay over the wheel, cigarette in his mouth and he just puffed away, only taking it out when he broke into song.

"Sure I love the dear silver that shines in your hair…
"Da da da, da da da da, da da da da da…"

By now, I was getting somewhat scunnered[†].

We eventually reached Westport and Jimmy continued down towards the quay, where he parked up and almost fell out of the van. I didn't get out but opened the door wide. He

---

[*] **Blueshirt**…*A member of an Irish fascist organisation, popular in the 1930s, modelled on Mosley's 'Blackshirts'.*
[†] **Scunnered**…*Ulster/Scots, totally fed up. Frustrated.*

went across into a small garage and spoke with a man who looked like he was the boss, or maybe the foreman, and while they talked, I could see Jimmy pointing back at the van. They spoke for a few minutes and, as I could see from his gesturing, Jimmy was explaining which wheel needed repairing. I kept watching and as Jimmy turned to come back to the van, the man called, "I'll have it sorted in no time, Jimmy." Jimmy signalled a thumbs-up.

As he approached the van, he nodded to somewhere down the street and said, "Come on wi' me, Frankie Boy."

I jumped out and we walked about a hundred yards, when suddenly I got the distinct waft of a fish-and-chip shop coming from somewhere. Jimmy rounded a corner with me in tow, and sure enough, there in front of us was a cafe. It was a sight for sore eyes I can tell you. Our order was taken the minute we sat down. As we waited to be served, my tummy was rumbling. Very soon, a girl with eye-catching red hair and an even more eye-catching miniskirt emerged from the kitchen carrying a tray laden with our order, and two well-stacked plates of fish and chips and peas were set in front of us. And to be fair to Jimmy, he paid for it.

"No, no, Frankie, put that back in your pocket. I'll get this, just you get stuck in!" he said, when he saw me pulling out my pound note.

So I did both, I put the pound back in my pocket and got stuck in. And very tasty it was too. Although, the deeper I got into it, the more I had a feeling that either the fish or the batter was a bit off…but I didn't let it bother me. I put it down to maybe being too hungry.

When the waitress came back to take our dessert order, Jimmy passed, while I chose apple tart and ice cream, not only because I fancied that dessert, but I fancied another glimpse of those long legs in that short skirt again. But I was to be disappointed when the girl who took my order came back with it.

While I was tucking in, Jimmy scraped the last piece of fish off his plate with his knife, downed the remainder of his milk and then wiped his mouth with his sleeve. Whether his mouth was cleaner or dirtier from the sleeve rub would be a hard one to guess. He then got up and went over to speak to a man who I presumed was the owner. While I couldn't hear what they were saying, the conversation looked a bit strained. After a moment or two, the two of them disappeared through a door over in the corner which said 'PRIVATE'. I finished my dessert and I was just sitting there, looking around and hoping to catch another glimpse of the red-haired cutty[*], when the private door opened. Jimmy emerged alone and without stopping at the table gave me a nod and a wink to get on my feet. I sprang up and followed him out. He wasn't staggering now, but walking briskly. He seemed in a bit of a hurry. I was curious as to why the big rush out, but I dared not ask him.

Are we doing a runner? I wondered for a moment. Had he paid for the meal at all?

When we got back to the garage, Jimmy first went into a shop next door and bought cigarettes and asked me if I wanted anything. I said no, I couldn't eat another bite.

The van was ready to go and the garage man says, "There was a hole in the tube and we patched it. But you'll need an exhaust, soon, Jimmy. I've fixed yours as best I could. It might do you a while."

---

[*] **Cutty**…*Ulster/Scots, a young girl, about teenage years.*

I couldn't believe my ears! Fixed exhaust! This garage man must know Jimmy well.

"What do I owe you?" says Jimmy, reaching into his pocket.

"Ah, sure thirty bob will do."

Jimmy reached into his hip pocket and produced some notes, gave him three ten-shilling notes and then shouted at the lad, "C'mere, boyo!" The 'boyo' this time was the lad who had helped fix the wheel. Jimmy reached into his trouser pocket and brought out a handful of change, from which he extracted two half-crowns* and, handing them to the lad, said, "That's for yourself. Now don't lose them."

The lad blushed. Then he beamed a big smile, looking up at the boss and then at the money in his hand again. I reckon the boss was his father and the lad was probably passing his school holidays, helping out.

I got in and Jimmy hauled himself up and, having squared himself in the seat, he turned the key, pulled the starter – and do you know what? It sounded like a new van – and no fumes. No more carbon monoxide, I hoped.

"That sorts out the slow puncture," says Jimmy. "A patch did the job."

Just at that moment, he let out another brattle of farts and said, "Oops." He looked over at me and said apologetically, "It's the tablets, Frankie, it's the tablets."

I looked back at him and said, "Jimmy, you should have got the man to put a patch on your arse as well."

He just smiled.

---

* **Half crown…***Pre decimalisation coin, then equal to two and a half shillings or, post decimalisation, 25p, about €2.00 today.*

The meal and glass of milk had sobered Jimmy up a little, and when we were well out of town, he said the trip to Westport was worthwhile, so I presumed he had either sold something or bought something. He paused for a bout of coughing, then continued, "Aye, it was a good stop." And then he leaned over towards me and dropped his voice. Why he did this, I couldn't tell you, as there were only the two of us in the van.

"You see that boyo in the chip shop back there?" he said, and then he paused, waiting for a comment from me.

After a pause I said, "Aye, so what about him?"

Jimmy tapped the outside of his coat and said with a serious look on his face, "He owed me money for over a year now, Frankie, and I thought I'd never get it. Fifty quid he owed me."

I didn't comment. It was none of my business. But he repeated, a little louder, "Fifty quid."

"See that fish you were eating," he went on. "That was mine. I supplied him with top-quality fish like that for nearly a year and he never feckin' paid me. Kept giving me the run around. Always promised he'd pay me next time. But I never give up! It's the Corkman in me."

With that, he reached into the inside pocket of his coat and produced a fistful of cash, all crumpled up in a mess, and waved it at me.

Whatever Jimmy lacked, it certainly wasn't tenacity. And at least we hadn't left without paying, which set my mind at rest.

"Look, Frankie, look at that," he said with a look of content, then went to put it back in his pocket. But then all of a sudden, he looked at me, and instead he handed the wad to me.

"Here, Frankie, sort that out and count it for me, just to be sure. I only gave it a rough count in the café. You'll be a better counter than me."

So I counted it on my knee.

It was a whole mixture of ten-shilling notes, one-pound notes, five-pound notes and one tenner, all greasy, with the smell of a fish-and-chip shop from them. But sure enough, when I got the notes straightened out, sorted right way round and counted, there was fifty pounds exactly in the lot. I folded them neatly and gave them back. He looked at the folded bundle and said, "Frankie, you'd make a quare banker, the way you counted that money," before lifting his backside up a little off the seat and stuffing the wad into his hip pocket.

I was actually quite used to this, as I had often helped out my father with the wages for the railway workers.

When he got the cash well stuffed in, I thought to myself, *Before the day's out, that money will soon lose the smell of fish and chips.*

"Sure that was definitely a worthwhile stop," he repeated, as he slapped the steering wheel. "To tell you the truth, Frankie, I had sort of half written it off. I was beginning to think I'd never get it. You know, Frankie, when you get money like that, money you thought you'd never see, sure it's like ye got it for nothing. But it's the last fish he'll get from me, I can tell you. He won't catch me again and that's for sure."

"It was definitely worthwhile then," I echoed.

With that, he tore the wrapping of the new cigarette packet, extracted one, tapped it on the box, one end, then the other, lit it and took a long draw. He always seemed to get great satisfaction from the first draw.

"Sure I love the dear silver that shines in your hair..."

The fifty pounds certainly added to his timbre and there was a definite uplift in his mood. Things were looking up, all in all. The van was quieter, Jimmy had got his long-awaited debt, the puncture was fixed, I was no longer hungry, and we were not a million miles away from County Cork. Not close, but closer anyway.

"Ohhhhhh, God bless you and keep you, Mother Machree."

Half an hour later, or maybe a bit more, we were going down through the beautiful Connemara, Leenaun and Maum, where John Wayne courted Maureen O'Hara and fought the bit out with Squire Danaher, all those years ago.

There wasn't a cloud in the sky.

Even as a seventeen-year-old, I could see why John Ford chose this location. It was truly magnificent. At Maam Cross, we turned left over the bridge, and we were on the road to Oughterard and the beautiful views over Lough Corrib. Halfway between Maam Cross and Oughterard, we passed a side road which had a signpost on which was written 'THE QUIET MAN BRIDGE', and an arrow pointing up the road. This was the bridge where Sean Thornton, played by John Wayne, sits and reminisces about his childhood and youth.

Echoing my thoughts, Jimmy said quietly, as if with reverence, "They made *The Quiet Man* around here, they did."

I just replied, "I know."

"Arragh, indeed they did. And John Wayne was here – and Mary O'Hara, too."

He was almost whispering.

"Maureen O'Hara," I said softly. I just couldn't help it.

"Aye, she was indeed," he said. I didn't go any further with that one. There was no point.

"I seen it twice, or maybe three times," he boasted.

"Aye, so did I," I countered.

I had watched the film a couple of times. It was a favourite of my mother and father's and was shown a few times on RTE.

The shimmering sun was glinting off the lake below us and I expected Jimmy any minute to break into a verse of 'The Isle of Inisfree' or 'The Wild Colonial Boy'.

But no, Jimmy remained faithful to Mother Machree.

"Sure I love the dear silver that shines in your hair…"

Soon, we left John Wayne and *The Quiet Man* behind us as we got closer to Galway. It was almost five o'clock when we reached the outskirts, and we were able to avoid the city by going round by Oranmore. With no delays, we were on the road to Limerick in no time. We stopped for a splash and a refill at a wee pub in Gort, where, although he bought himself the usual beverage, I passed. For a change, we didn't spend too long as, luckily, Jimmy didn't know the barman and, even luckier for the barman, he didn't know Jimmy. So he drank up fairly quickly and we got aboard once again.

I had long come to the conclusion that the crabs, or whatever they were, didn't need the moistening as much as

43

Jimmy. Like me, they probably just needed a breath of fresh air.

I guessed we'd reach Limerick about six o'clock and I remember saying to myself, *I bet he stops at Durty Nelly's*, a well-known wee pub just beside Bunratty Castle and not too far from Shannon Airport. It was just typical of the kind of place Jimmy would frequent. He probably knew Durty Nelly – and maybe she knew Durty Jimmy!

On previous journeys with my father, we had stopped there a couple of times and I can guarantee that whoever did the cooking could certainly make a bowl of soup. And you got as much home-made wheaten bread and butter as you wanted. And an ice-cold Fanta. And I remember a hippy kind of boy, long hair and beard, playing an accordion in the corner and singing traditional Irish songs. *He'll hardly be there now*, I thought. *He's probably moved on.*

I suppose, on reflection, I knew it was hardly Durty Nelly who made the soup, seeing as she had died about three hundred years ago. Now whether it was called Durty Nelly's because Nelly was 'durty' or the pub was 'durty', who knows, but I remember from previous visits, the door was so small you could have banged your head on the lintel on the way in. And if you did, you remembered on the way out. I knew this for a fact!

Despite my memories, I really didn't want him to stop anywhere, I just wanted to get to Fermoy. The thought of Durty Nelly's soup didn't really appeal to me by that stage, anyway, so I told myself that I wouldn't mention the place and hoped Jimmy would just drive on.

But then, just as we entered Ennis, nightmare of all nightmares, Jimmy said, sort of apologetically, "Just one more quick call, Frankie, I have to go down to Kilrush."

Jesus, I thought, *Durty Nelly's would have been a better option!*

So, it was a right at the traffic lights in Ennis and we were on the road west out of town.

Sure what could I do about it, anyway? I was stuck with him now!

Somewhere between Ennis and Kilrush on a lonely stretch of road, we stopped at a small pub for another watering, both in and out. However, in answer to Jimmy's question, the young girl behind the counter replied that the boss was away for the day. So there was very little conversation. Jimmy drank up, we made a quick visit to the toilets. On the way out, Jimmy asked the girl if it was okay to get some water from the tap outside.

"Yes, of course," she replied, but when we turned on the tap, no water emerged. Jimmy threw the empty drum back into the van and said that we would be okay until we reached Kilrush.

Before he got back in, Jimmy kicked the recently fixed wheel. Thankfully, the boyo's handiwork held out and the tyre was staying up. For a change, everything was airtight – at least as far as the van was concerned.

Eventually, we reached Kilrush about five thirty, having briefly stopped at a filling station for more petrol just outside the town.

Naturally he pulled up at the pier and got talking to a few fishermen. It was handshakes all round. *Jesus*, I thought, *is there anybody in Ireland that doesn't know Jimmy?* After the greetings, they all turned and walked into a large shed, which I assumed was some sort of a fish market, as a forklift was continually on the move, in and out, loaded with fish boxes. Jimmy probably went in with the others to look at the day's catch. I sat in the van, wondering how long he'd be.

I could see a phone box about a hundred and fifty yards away and the thought of calling home occurred to me. But these were the days before automatic dialling and to get a call through from Kilrush to Carrigans could take anything from five minutes to half an hour – or more, depending on the mood of those operating the various exchanges along the way. And then the thought occurred to me that while I was in the phone box, what if Jimmy came back and forgot all about me and drove off?

So I abandoned the idea and, anyway, sure it wouldn't be long now until we reached Fermoy. So I just sat tight.

I closed my eyes for just a moment.

Next thing the blast of a car horn nearby wakened me. I had fallen asleep. As I had no watch, I couldn't tell how long I'd been out, but I guessed about fifteen or twenty minutes. Then, spying a street pump across the way, it occurred to me that I might as well fill the drum while Jimmy was in the fish store.

So I did. I took it out, refilled it, and put it back in and closed the back doors. At least that was that sorted. By now, I was highly proficient at filling water drums!

After I put the drum back, I wandered up towards the fish store, hoping he would see me and get a move on. On the way I managed to find a public toilet that was actually quite clean. I did what I had to do, came out of the toilets and went into the big shed. But when I walked in, the place was empty. No fishermen, no fish and – surprise, surprise – no Jimmy! Even the forklift man had disappeared, his machine parked in the corner. Immediately my suspicions were coming to the fore and I turned and walked outside and looked up the street. Just as I guessed, there was a pub about a hundred yards away. I started to walk towards it.

As I got closer, I bet myself my own pound note that Jimmy would be ensconced inside.

I might have known!

Sure enough, there he was, holding court at the bar with three or four other men, talking away. He had a cigarette in his mouth and on the counter in front of him stood a half of whiskey and a glass of Guinness.

When I saw him there, I was beside myself and for the one and only time, I raised my voice.

"Jimmy, come on, *please*! My father and mother will be worried sick about me."

With an emphasis on the "please".

The minute I had said it, I was sorry I had spoken. You could have heard a pin drop.

They all turned round to look at me and I was expecting Jimmy to blow a gasket or something, but after a second, he looked at me and just muttered, "Right, right". As he drank up, he bid his farewell to the barman and the others, left his glass gently on the counter and followed me out. He practically fell out the door, having misjudged the step. He looked at his watch and in mock surprise, said, "Bejaysus, look at the time, Frankie. Sure I didn't think it was that time."

Like hell he didn't!

"Will you fill the jar, Frankie Boy?" He staggered towards the van.

"I've already filled it, Jimmy. We're all done and ready to go."

"Fair play to ye, Frankie, you're a grand lad," he said, as he took about three efforts to get himself into the van. "So now, Frankie, it's next stop – Fermoy."

I'll believe it when we get there, I thought.

"Sure I love the dear silver…"

But that didn't last long. He just managed the first couple of words.

We left Kilrush and drove to Killimer, where we caught the ferry across the Shannon to Tarbert. We sat in the van during the crossing and Jimmy fell asleep. Any thoughts I had of sleeping were scuppered by his snoring. Eventually the Tarbert slipway came into view, the bow door was lowered, and the ferry came to a grinding stop as the door and concrete met. The tannoy announced our arrival – as if we didn't know.

We were parked about halfway back in the boat, so I called, "C'mon, Jimmy, waken up," and gave him a dig with my hand. He half wakened but by the time it was our turn to move, he was fully awake, but in bad shape with the drink.

He also let go another plume of methane, looked at me and said quietly, "It's the tablets, Frankie, it's the tablets."

I couldn't even open the window, nor could I open the door as there was a car parked close to us. If anyone needed tablets at that stage, it was me.

I feared it would be touch and go whether he would be able to complete the journey or not. But we got on to the main road, through Tarbert Town, and headed south through Listowel, Tralee, and then into Killarney, in County Kerry.

"If ye weren't with me, Frankie, I'd be taking that road to Cork," he said, pointing right at a junction. "But sure Fermoy is not too far out of the way and I'll take you there, so I will."

At that moment, I was sorry for shouting at him in Kilrush. But I said nothing.

I had got used to saying nothing.

It was by now almost nine o'clock and the daylight was beginning to fade just a little. In Killarney there were crowds of people on the street, many sitting outside bars, having a drink. Probably all tourists, I reckoned. There was singing in almost every pub and bar, backed by every kind of musical instrument, from fiddles to accordions, bodhráns to tin whistles. There was music of all kinds coming at us, each tune merging into another, as we drove through the town. The street was brightly lit and there was definitely a holiday atmosphere. Jimmy had his window down and he waved at anyone who looked in his direction. I think he was pretending to me that these folks all knew him and he knew them.

But in no time at all, it seemed, the lights and the crowds, the fiddles, the accordions and the bodhráns all faded away, and we left Killarney behind us.

We were on the dark and lonely road again, heading for Mallow.

Nearly there, I thought, more in hope than expectation.

"... Ohhhhhh, God bless you and keep you, Mother Machree."

The conversation dried up somewhat. I was very tired and not feeling great – I could sense that the fish in the café in Westport was beginning to retaliate. I hoped I could make it to Fermoy without being sick, but the odds weren't looking too good. Jimmy was singing very low to himself and after a long and thankfully uneventful stretch of the journey, we reached Mallow, getting there at about ten o'clock. Jimmy was now driving very slowly. He couldn't but drive slowly anyway, as one of his headlights was not working and the other was no better than the lamp on my bicycle at home. He nearly fell asleep again a couple of times. I had to keep a close watch on him. As well, the exhaust patch was coming loose and the gas was leaking again. And the methane gauge was rising, too. I was starting to feel seriously sick and everything was beginning to point in one direction.

The streets in Mallow were dead, compared to Killarney. There was hardly a soul about. In fact, it all looked a bit eerie. A heavy fog, maybe more of a smog, began to form in the streets, which reminded me of those old black-and-white horror films. I feared that this would delay us even more, but as we left town it lifted with a soft breeze as suddenly as it had dropped, and was gone.

But the smog in my tummy wasn't lifting and eventually, a couple of miles out of Mallow, I knew that I couldn't hold out any longer. Seeing a dimly lit 'GUINNESS' sign and the lights of a pub ahead, I told Jimmy that I needed to stop – *"NOW!"*

I felt my tummy about to explode, so he pulled into the car park across the road from the bar. The catalyst was an extremely long emission from Jimmy, which I don't think he even realised he had jettisoned. I wondered how many tablets he could blame for that one!

I opened the door and was out and, even before he had brought the van to a stop, I was leaning against it and decorating the car park with fish and chips, apple tart, milk and Football Special, and topping it all off with a mosaic of peas. And trying my best to keep it off my clothes and shoes.

Jimmy staggered out of the van and peeped round.

"Are ye all right there, Frankie?" he asked and then added as an afterthought, "Was it something ye ate, do ye think?"

Jesus Christ, what a question to ask, I thought to myself as I heaved up what was left.

"I suppose so, must have been," I muttered, as I straightened up and did my best to clean myself with the handkerchief my mother had given me that morning.

Morning seemed a long time ago.

"Are ye okay, Frankie?" he again asked quietly. I suppose he meant well and there was no point in mentioning the fact that the cigarettes, the mixture of gases, especially his, and the bouncing of the old van didn't help the situation. And I felt like telling him that it was no wonder the man in Westport didn't pay him for the fish – it was fucking rotten! I wouldn't have paid him for it either. We *should* have done a runner.

But I held my tongue. Again.

After a few minutes walking around the car park, I felt a bit better. I just had to get it all up.

Jimmy made as if to go to the back of the van, but I said to him, "Get you into the van and I'll do the water." I was afraid he would disappear across the road into the pub, so I kept my eye on him. But this time, he didn't argue. He opened the passenger door of the van and, reaching into the glove compartment, pulled out a half pint glass from among a bundle of old papers and receipts. After I filled the bucket, he rinsed the glass in the bucket, then filled it with water and drank it back in one go. He filled it again and downed that as well.

"Ah, that's better," he said, before bringing his sleeve into play. After giving the glass a shake to ensure it was empty, he offered it to me without speaking. Not surprisingly, I declined. He returned the glass to the glove compartment, turned and went round to the driver's side and struggled back into the van.

I opened the back doors, got the slack one jammed open with a stick and, with just one throw this time, I splashed the crates. I didn't really care how much water went in. But I left the drum half full, in case he needed it after I left him in Fermoy. I poured a little into the bucket for a drink for myself to take away the bad taste. I didn't swallow – just rinsed my mouth before spitting it out and then wiping my mouth with the last clean corner of my handkerchief. By that stage the hankie was in bad shape also. It wasn't worth holding on to, so I threw it into the hedge.

I stood for moment, just to settle myself and then, having replaced the drum and bucket, closed up the doors and got back into the van. But when I looked across, I saw that Jimmy was asleep at the wheel – literally.

I gave him a gentle shake and he immediately straightened up with a start, looked at me as if he'd never seen me before and said, "Right, right."

After a moment he got his bearings and, firing the engine, he pulled the gear stick towards him and down and managed to get into first without effort. He was still not fully awake and he didn't really know where he was for a moment or two. But after I kept talking to him for a few seconds, he came round and soon we were back on the straight and narrow.

"Sure we're nearly there, Frankie, nearly there now," he said very quietly. Then he began to hum Mother Machree. It was all he could manage now, but it soon faded and he was quiet.

I don't think he had a clue where he was. He was on autopilot. It was now a question of keeping him awake. So I kept talking to him about everything and anything, just to make sure he stayed alert. But when he began to say something, he would get quieter, until the sentence just faded out without an end. Then after a minute, he would say something else. To be fair, he did brighten up a bit as we went on. The two glasses of water had obviously helped. Jimmy had been out before.

I thought Fermoy was never going to arrive, but soon we were in the village of Ballyhooley, where the street takes a ninety-degree right then a ninety-degree left, which I thought he'd never manoeuvre. But he managed both turns without clipping a kerb or, worse still, going straight through the wall at the first turn and ending up in the cemetery on the other side. At the end of the street, we were back in the countryside and as we left the village I knew that, finally, Fermoy was not far away.

Just another couple of miles and I just couldn't wait!

Jimmy asked where my father was staying and I told him the Royal Hotel, in the Square.

Ten minutes later, we crossed the Blackwater bridge and pulled into the Square. I had finally arrived – at long last. It was almost a quarter to eleven. I had been on the road since five thirty that morning. Over seventeen hours. And I had been in nine counties of Ireland!

"There you are now, Frankie," he said. "Didn't we get here in the end and sure didn't the day pass quick enough!"

That's a statement if ever I heard one, I thought to myself. I didn't know if he was being serious or just joking. Then he looked at me with a serious face.

"By the way, Frankie, I didn't get your second name?"

"McGurk," I said, as I opened the door. I got out and reached back in for my coat and duffel bag. I intended to walk around to his side to thank him and say goodbye, but he had also climbed out and had managed to come round to my side. The van stood between us and the hotel.

"Good luck now, Frankie McGurk, good luck to ye. It was a pleasure having you along. Sure maybe we'll do it again sometime!" he said with a smile. He stood close to me and the smell of drink from him was almost making me sick again.

He clasped my hand, shook it and slapped my shoulder with his other hand. I could feel something against my palm. When he took his hand away, I opened mine and there, like a butterfly opening its wings, was a five-pound note, folded twice. He must have been holding it in his hand for ages.

Five pounds was a fortune in 1969, even if it did have a waft of methane from it.

I looked up and said, "No, Jimmy, I can't take that."

I offered it back to him, but he put his hands up and shook his head.

"No, no, sure I couldn't have managed without ye. Ye kept me going when I was tired, and ye helped me with the water and all that. Arragh, Frankie, you're a grand lad, aye, a grand lad and you were great company. Look after yourself now!"

And then he turned and staggered round to the driver's side of the van. He could hardly manage it, but he eventually hauled himself in and with another rasp of the gearstick and a puff of smoke, he gave the engine a rev up and, turning right, drove out of the Square. As he made the turn, he waved out the window, beeped the horn and called back, "Good luck to ye, Frankie."

I wondered for a moment how he would ever reach Cork by himself. I tried to think of something to call to him but I couldn't find the right words, so I just waved at him and said, "Bye, Jimmy – and thanks."

But he wouldn't have heard it anyway. I listened for some time to the sound of the van as it echoed through the empty streets, until the sound slowly faded away in the distance and then, silence.

Jimmy was finally gone.

I thought for a moment I could hear 'Mother Machree', but I knew it was just my imagination.

Then I suddenly realised – he really is gone, and this time for good. I just stood there and thought I'll probably never see him again in my life. And I never did. Then it hit me that I forgot to ask him what his surname was. All I knew was that he was Jimmy. Despite many efforts recently, with the availability of email, internet, etc., the bould Jimmy has eluded me. I never did manage to track him down.

Too late now. As old Rose said in the film 'Titanic', "he exists now only in my memory."

It's more than likely Jimmy has gone to his rest. If he has, I could nearly bet what they sang at his funeral...And I smile sometimes, thinking that if I had my way, I know what I'd put on his headstone:

But I'll never forget Jimmy or the day we spent together, over fifty years ago, looking back now, almost a lifetime. Yet in another way, it seems just like yesterday. And I have retraced that journey a thousand times, in my mind, over those many years.

I often promised myself, years ago, that I would drive it all again sometime. Maybe take herself and the kids, and then years later, it was maybe take herself and the grandkids.

But I never did. And probably never will now.

All I have now are the memories.

But I remember them all clearly, the starts and the stops, the detours, the splashes and slashes, the laughs, the carbon monoxide and the methane. The Guinness and the whiskey and the Football Specials, and the fish, chips and peas, even if they did end up all over a car park, somewhere in County Cork.

What a story!

And of course, while the main players were Jimmy and me, the cast included Lord Mountbatten, W.B. Yeats, John Wayne and Maureen O'Hara, and a host of others. Sure didn't they all have a small part, even if they didn't know it at the time?

And, of course, Mother Machree.

As I stood in the quietness of the Square, I looked at the five-pound note again and, strange as it might sound, I felt a lump in my throat. Why, I'm not sure. I folded it back the way Jimmy had done and slipped it into my hip pocket.

Then I looked across at the hotel and lo and behold there stood my father at the front door.

I can still see him to this day, immaculately dressed as he always was, in shirt and tie and jacket, perfectly creased trousers and shoes polished. Then, for some inexplicable reason – but I suppose, looking back now it is obvious what the reason was – the lump in my throat got bigger, the tears welled up and despite my best efforts to hold back, I started to cry, right there on the street. I suppose it was a combination of everything that day and now seeing my father, standing there at the door.

And the tears didn't half flow. It felt as if I hadn't seen him for years!

I walked, then broke into a run towards him and he put his arms around me. It wasn't something he had done since I was a wee boy. What teenager wants his father to hug him, especially in public? But I didn't care who saw us that night, I was so relieved to see him and, probably more so, he to see me.

I couldn't hug him enough.

"Come on, come on, you're okay," he said, in an effort to calm me down. I can still hear his soft voice.

The tears just kept flowing.

I could smell the Brylcreem he always used, off him and it was an indescribable change from what I had experienced all day. The scent of that particular hair cream *was* my father.

It was ingrained in my DNA for seventeen years. And still is to this very day.

I asked him for his handkerchief, as mine, the one my mother had given me that morning, was gone. It had fought a long and brave battle that day – well above and beyond the call of duty – but eventually it succumbed to superior forces and ended up in a hedge somewhere between Mallow and Fermoy.

After a minute or so, I dried up the tears and, swinging the duffel bag over my shoulder, we walked into the hotel together.

"Your Mammy and I were worried about you," he said quietly and, in the light of the hotel lobby, I could see the relief in his eyes.

Just as we reached the reception desk, the girl said, "Mr. McGurk, call for you."

He took the receiver at the desk and it was my mother. Apparently, she had been phoning continuously throughout the evening and night.

My father said, "Yes, yes, he's just come in. Here he is, hold on."

He handed me the phone.

My mother kept asking if I was alright. She was thanking God and all the saints and telling me to be sure to say my prayers before I went to bed, especially thanking St. Joseph. I assured her I would and after a few more words we said goodbye. I suppose I didn't understand then what they were so worried about. But I do now.

My father looked at me and he said, "Are you hungry, son?"

"No, I'm okay, just tired, very tired. I had a bite not too long ago."

There was no need to get into the detail about the food, at that stage. I didn't even want to think about food. It would all keep until tomorrow. All I wanted was a nice clean warm bed to lie down in – and a long, long sleep.

"You were a long time on the road, today," he said, as we walked towards the stairs.

"Indeed I was."

"Boysaboys – you didn't get too many lifts then?"

"No," says I… "Just the one."

Mother Machree

There's a spot in my heart, which no colleen may own.
There's a depth in my soul, never sounded or known.
There's a place in my mem'ry, my life, that you fill,
No other can take it, no-one ever will...

Sure, I love the dear silver that shines in your hair,
And the brow that's all furrowed, and wrinkled with care.
I kiss the dear fingers, so toil-worn for me...Ohhhhh,
God bless you and keep you, Mother Machree.

Ev'ry sorrow or care in the dear days gone by,
Was made bright by the light of the smile in your eye,
Like a candle that's set in the window at night
Your fond love has cheered me and guided me right...

Sure, I love the dear silver that shines in your hair,
And the brow that's all furrowed, and wrinkled with care.
I kiss the dear fingers, so toil-worn for me...Ohhhhh,
God bless you and keep you, Mother Machree.

2

Aces and Eights

The owner of a public house is in breach of the law
Or is he...?

Apparently, Wild Bill Hickok was holding a poker hand of two pair, aces and eights, all black, when he was murdered by Jack McCall in Deadwood, Dakota, in 1876. Whether he really had what is still called a 'dead man's hand' or whether this is just another in a long list of legends concerning the Old West is neither here nor there. But in John Martin's poker machine, if you were lucky enough to get two pair, be they aces and eights or in fact any two pair, it was good luck as, no matter what the combination, two pair rattled out your winnings. Not a lot, but enough to keep you tempted to have another go.

As far away as you could get from Deadwood, just beside the beach, on the shores of Lough Foyle, at a place called Magilligan Point, near Limavady in Northern Ireland, my father once owned a small public house.

It was simply called the Point Bar.

We didn't work in the pub ourselves. My father had a local couple, John and Marie Martin, running the business as tenants. But it was far from being a money-making enterprise. It was totally dependent on the summer trade, and then only when the weather was good. Unlike local pubs in towns and villages, which in general have the same customers all year round, our pub was very much dependent on the tourist industry.

The upside was that, despite the summer being relatively short, when the weather was good, trade was indeed good, and closing time at night was fairly flexible as the police seldom visited. And the very few times they did, it was just to ask something like, "Is it not time you got the doors closed, John?" This could have been 2 a.m.! John was well known and, apart from being a little slack with his opening and closing hours, the pub didn't cause any trouble so the police were never too hard on him. They knew that his season was short, and therefore he had to make the best of it. So, as long as there were no complaints, the police generally turned a blind eye to the clock.

During the winter months, the pub remained closed and shuttered and few people came to Magilligan Point – perhaps a couple giving their dog a walk on the beach, or someone keen on a bit of winter windsurfing. It was a bleak place at that time of year and, like daffodils, only came to life with the coming of spring.

John and Marie would open around Easter and close in early September.

At that time, we also had a salmon fishery on the beach, and it took a crew of about six or seven men, including myself, to work it. When the fishing season was operating – approximately through the months of June, July and the first half of August – the crew including myself stayed in a small cottage, which we called 'the fishermen's hut' and which stood about twenty yards from the public house.

Several people from different parts of the country brought their caravans and boats to Magilligan Point during those summer months. And so between the fishermen making their annual visit, the arrival, like swallows, of the caravan visitors, and the pub opening, life once again blossomed for a couple of months at 'the Point'.

And the Point Bar was the hub of the activities.

John and Marie Martin had a daughter called Morac, who was about four years of age in 1984, the year of this story.

Technically, John Martin was managing the pub, but he just paid my father an agreed fixed amount every week and what he and Marie made on top of that, they kept. That was the deal.

John and Marie were and still are a very good couple, hard-working, and both of them having a quick wit – something which was vital to run a public house. Unfortunately, their daughter, Morac, developed bad health when she was a child and it plagued her incessantly, until she finally died, aged just thirty-seven, in 2017. She was their only child. They have never got over it, naturally.

But during the good days, we had some great 'craic' at the Point Bar. For instance, on several Monday nights, we used to hold a 'disco'. But not a proper one with electronic strobe lights, etc. Our disco consisted of a jukebox, or, as John Martin called it, the 'jutebox', blaring old singles, the main lights switched off and me sitting on a high stool flashing a torch, or maybe two, at the ceiling, while the rest of the customers danced to the music. The jukebox only had about five or six records in at any time, so it was the same songs again and again!

John Martin used to always name things incorrectly on purpose. As I have said, he called the jukebox a 'jutebox'. A 'barbeque' was a 'barleyque' and a rubber dinghy was a 'Robey Dingey'.

In the lounge, he had a pool table and Liam 'the Ganch' Doherty was by far the best pool player. (A 'ganch' is an Ulster-Scots term for a person who never stops talking.) So on a few Monday nights, when we weren't discoing, Liam used to shout, "Right, everyone! Pool competition. One-pound entry and large fresh salmon for the winner."

So everybody would give a pound and whoever won the pool tournament would get a fresh salmon – if they wanted it. A few locals might have been about, so if the Ganch collected, say, ten players at a pound per entrant, that totalled a tenner. That's about what I would charge for the average-sized salmon. Liam would inevitably win the competition, but he had no interest in an eight-pound salmon, whereupon he would sell the salmon back to me for, say, five pounds. So I was in a fiver, he was in a fiver and I still had the salmon! It was a good laugh. Worth every pound and everyone was a winner. Especially Liam!

To boost his income, John had brought a poker machine into the bar, which was of course illegal. I never discussed it with my father. We had no idea if it was legal or not, nor did we care. My father asked no questions. John didn't mention it either – one day it just appeared.

I think my father's attitude was, well if John Martin wants to take a chance, it's his decision. Although illegal, many small country pubs did have one, which the police generally ignored. They had enough on their plate at that time. The machine in our bar stood half-hidden behind a jukebox. It was a fifty-pence slot one and if you hit the jackpot, a Royal Flush, it paid out handsomely. If memory serves me right, a Royal Flush got you five hundred quid. But you needed a bit of good luck to get any more out of the machine than you put in. Of course, if it worked the other way round, sure it would be no use to John Martin, would it?

But while it may have only on very rare occasions paid out a big jackpot like a Royal Flush, it often paid out smaller amounts. For John and Marie, it was a money-spinner.

Mostly you got just a pair of twos, or a pair of anything, which, at least, paid you back your fifty pence, the lowest amount of winnings, which, of course, you re-slotted until you lost, or hit the jackpot. But that's the nature of gambling.

I never really understood how gambling could consume a man until we got to see the same clients in the bar, having changed their wages into fifty-pence pieces before arriving, then slotting them all into the machine in the hope of the elusive Royal Flush. One coin after another, with pay-outs rare. And in no time the punter's fifty-pence pieces – their week's wages – were gone.

In the long run, in any form of gambling, the punter always loses. John's poker machine was no different. At the end of the day, John and Marie Martin were the only winners.

I suppose it was just another version of a one-armed-bandit. But I've seen players who, having had a hand of black aces and eights turn up on the machine, played no more, drank up and left, their superstitions aroused by the old 'dead man's hand'. Aces and eights.

One day in July, during that good summer of '84 if I remember correctly, about late morning or thereabouts, a local man who was a friend of John Martin, named Kevin

Boucher [pronounced 'Butcher'] was behind the bar, filling in as barman for that particular day. John and Marie had taken the day off and, with little Morac, they were enjoying the festival in Moville, a seaside town across in Donegal.

As Kevin later recalled, there were no customers in the bar. Just a couple of the fishing crew playing pool in the lounge as they waited for the tide to turn, when we would don our gear, load up the DUKW and head for the shore to cast our nets. The DUKW was a World War II amphibious craft, which was ideal for our type of fishing. Our fishing times depended on the tides.

A couple of the fishing crew and myself were repairing a few holes in the net, just between the fishermen's hut and the pub, when a car pulled up outside the bar. A couple emerged from the vehicle, he was about forty-five, she was about thirty, both well dressed, and walked into the bar. While we did see them going into the bar, we didn't give them a second thought.

Kevin later told us that when they entered he remarked that the lady was quite attractive, slim with long blonde hair, and his first thought was that this was a couple meeting on the QT. A lovers' tryst, more than likely, he reckoned.

Not an uncommon event at the Point Bar, being off the beaten track. The couple took a seat in the far corner and then the man approached the bar and ordered a couple of soft drinks. He returned to the corner and sat down, and they talked in low whispers while they sipped.

Definitely, Kevin later said, he presumed they were a married couple (but not to each other). At some stage, the man got up and headed to the toilet. As he passed the poker machine, which was half-hidden by the jukebox, he pulled two or three fifty-pence pieces from his pocket, Kevin recalled, pushed them into the slot and pushed the button. But he had no luck. After he emerged from the toilets, they finished up their drinks, thanked Kevin and left.

About half an hour later, I was in the fishermen's hut – we were all getting a quick last bite before heading out to fish – when I spied Kevin running as fast as he could across the yard, into the hut, gasping.

He looked at me. "Quick, quick, Frank. You're wanted on the phone – right now!"

So, wondering if there was something wrong at home, I ran as fast as I could across the yard, in through the front door of the bar, ducked under the counter hatch and grabbed the phone.

"Hello," I said, practically out of breath.

A voice said, "You're going to be raided in fifteen minutes and the poker machine seized."

Then the line went dead. That was it.

I did a bit of quick thinking and called to a couple of the boys, who had followed out of curiosity. "Right, quick boys. Give me a lift."

So three or four of us lifted the poker machine and carried it out of the bar. But not before Kevin took a key from his pocket, opened a small door at the rear of the machine, withdrew a money-drop basket, emptied all the fifty-pence pieces into a plastic bucket (except about a dozen coins, which he left), replaced the basket and locked the little door again. There must have been five hundred pounds in that basket.

We lifted the machine again and it did seem a good bit lighter and we carried it outside. I had decided to hide it in the fishermen's hut, but then changed my mind and called to one of the boys to open the back door of my van. Which he did.

We slid the poker machine in on its back and shut the back door again. In the meantime, Kevin had placed a table and chairs in the spot where the poker machine had stood. A pack of cards was produced and soon there were three or four of us, all sitting down, playing rummy.

Poker machine? What poker machine?

Not five minutes later, a large green van pulled into the yard and we could see out the window that there were two uniformed policemen aboard. We had just made it in time.

They didn't alight, but just sat in their van. We had a good idea who was coming next.

Sure enough, about fifteen minutes later, we heard a car pull up outside and a couple entered. It was, as we suspected, the same couple who had been in earlier. Kevin asked them something like, "Ah, you're back. Have you forgotten something, folks?"

"No," said the man. "We're police officers, my name is Inspector Ian Johnston, this is Sergeant Crawford." Both of them flashed their ID at the same time.

"And your name, sir?" the inspector asked, as the sergeant took her notebook from her handbag, folded it open and began taking notes.

"Kevin Boucher," says Kevin. "B-O-U-C-H-E-R." The sergeant began writing.

"Are you the manager, here?" the inspector asked.

"No," says Kevin. "The manager is John Martin."

"Is Mr. Martin here, then?"

"No, he's taken the day off today. I'm just helping out while he's away. Why, what's wrong?" asks Kevin.

"We are here to impound a poker gambling machine, which is illegal under the Gaming, Betting and Lotteries Act, 19 *whatever-the-year*" (or words to that effect).

As he spoke, the sergeant just stood there, writing away. Once she glanced round at us and I smiled at her. But she did not smile back and just gave me a very cold look.

Sourpuss, I thought to myself.

As the inspector was speaking to Kevin, the two burly policemen in uniform stepped out of their van and entered the bar. They removed their caps, setting them on the counter. They were here to do the heavy lifting – literally.

Looking back at the inspector, Kevin asks with an astonished look on his face, "What poker machine?"

The sergeant turned round, at the same time pointing at the spot where the jukebox had stood earlier.

"That one…" she said, but her jaw literally dropped when she saw it was not there. An equally puzzled look of amazement came over the inspector's face.

There was no poker machine. Just three or four lads playing cards.

The inspector turned back to Kevin and, pointing at the spot where we were playing cards at the table, said, "Okay, Mr. Boucher, where's the poker machine that was standing there an hour ago, behind that jukebox?"

No-one spoke for a moment.

Kevin shrugged his shoulders. "I don't know what you're talking about."

The sergeant spoke then. She couldn't hide her anger.

"Mr. Boucher, I hope you realise how serious a position you are leaving yourself in. We both saw it in here last time

69

we were in, and yet you deny that a machine stood there an hour ago?"

I remember thinking at the time that she was obviously not local, as she spoke with a soft English accent, uncannily like the actress Joanna Lumley. Kevin didn't answer her. She looked around at us again, but this time her face was red with rage.

I was going to smile at her again, but then I thought better of it and kept a straight face. The inspector then produced a sheet of paper, set it on the counter facing Kevin and said, "This is a search warrant. As you can see, it allows us to search the premises."

He had covered all angles. But at the same time, I wondered how much latitude the warrant gave him. Could he search the fisherman's hut, or the old tractor shed, or the small fuel shed? Or even my van? Or was it limited to the licensed premises?

Kevin says, without looking at it, "Okay, search away."

The inspector looked at the uniformed policemen and nodded his head. The two policemen then proceeded to search every room, upstairs, downstairs. Every nook and cranny.

While they did so, the inspector said something else to Kevin, while Sourpuss began asking names of those of us sitting round the card table. When she got to me, I just said, "Frank McGurk."

"Are you the owner?" she asked. She had obviously done her homework.

"No," says I. "That would be my father."

Eventually the heavy gang came back and one of them said, "No poker machine here, sir."

The inspector turned to me and said, "Mr. McGurk, can you step outside, please?"

I led the way out the door. He followed, but Sourpuss stayed behind, as did the two uniformed officers. When we had walked some yards away from the building, he said, "And what's your name, sir?"

"McGurk."

The inspector looked at me with some exasperation. "Yes, I know that much, I mean what's your first name?"

I said, "Frank."

He wrote it down.

"Well, Mr. McGurk, both you and I know that there was a poker machine in there earlier today and indeed it has been there for several weeks. But it's not you I need to speak with. It's your father, as you will understand. He is the licence holder of the premises. Is that correct?"

"Yes, sir, that is correct."

With that, he pulled a card from his breast pocket, handed it to me and said, "Please inform your father to call me tomorrow on this number. I'll be available all day."

I took the card, looked at it and saw that it said *Inspector Ian Johnston, RUC Station, Ballymena*, with the address below. A telephone number was displayed in the bottom corner. Obviously, in those days there was no email address or mobile number. Just a landline number.

"He will know the code for Ballymena, I presume?"

"Yes, he will," I said as I slipped it into my pocket.

"He regularly calls a business associate from Ballymena," I added, as he went to turn away.

"Does he now? And who would that be?"

I mentioned the name of a prominent businessman from Ballymena, who my father did business with some years previously, but not recently. I suppose I thought a bit of name-dropping might help.

"He hasn't called him in a while then," he commented after a few moments.

"How's that?" I said, somewhat puzzled.

"Because that man's been dead for about ten years." He walked back into the bar.

Shit, I thought to myself. I remained outside, cursing myself for putting my big foot in it.

A few moments later, the plain-clothes officers appeared and walked to their car. Sourpuss went to the driver's side. The inspector opened the door on the passenger side, then looked round at the fishermen's hut, just twenty yards away, saw the smoke emerging from the chimney and said to me, "Who lives in there?"

I said, "We do. The fishermen, sir."

He thought for a moment, then said, "Is it your house?"

I said, "Yes. Well actually no, it's my father's as well. The fishing crew stay there during the fishing season."

"Do you mind if we take a look in there?"

"For the poker machine?"

"No, not in particular," he replied, before adding, "Why, is it in there?"

I reckoned he thought he had us by the short and curlies. Even Sourpuss began to get a smell of victory.

I said, "Inspector, I'm not trying to be smart, but does that search warrant you have allow you to search the fishermen's hut too?"

As soon as I said it, I knew that it was the wrong thing to say. I'd just put my other foot in it. But my intention was to keep him away from the van at any cost. He said, curtly, "No, it doesn't, but I'll have one within the hour, if necessary."

I said, "Look, sir, I'm sorry. I have no problem if you want to look in there. You don't need a warrant. Look away, go ahead."

He stood for a moment, said something to Sourpuss. She replied but I didn't hear what she said, and then he said to me, "Okay, Mr. McGurk, that will be all for now. We may be back."

"Goodbye," I said.

Neither replied. They got into their car and drove off, but not before speaking with the uniformed men, who then got back into the big green van and followed them. Sourpuss, as she got into the car, gave me the foulest look I have ever got from anyone. I remember thinking, *I wouldn't want to fall out with you, Missus.*

I reciprocated with another smile, which she obviously wasn't impressed with. Her scowl only worsened. But then, that was my intention.

The excitement was over – for now.

After they disappeared, I ran up to the top of the hill behind the fishermen's hut and could see the green van and the car both disappear into the distance. After five minutes and another look, I decided to drive to one of the boy's home and leave the poker machine there. Just in case the boyos returned again for another search with a new bundle of warrants. But then I changed my mind. What if we met them, or were stopped up the road? So I dismissed that plan there and then.

But as soon as I did, another one formed.

I quickly jumped into the van, called for a couple of the boys to hop in as well, and I drove up round to the Martello Tower, about a hundred yards away. We carried the poker machine into a little WW2 ammunition store nearby, which was empty. We returned to the yard and parked the van in the same place.

It struck me afterwards that if we had taken the machine into the fishermen's hut, they probably couldn't have done anything about it. For one, they couldn't prove that the machine we might have had in the hut was the same one they saw in the bar earlier, and two, having a poker machine in a private house was probably not illegal anyway, I thought.

When they were well gone, I went back into the bar, phoned my father and told him the story. I didn't hold anything back, about the poker machine or us removing it, but I told him not to admit knowledge of the machine, at all, when he spoke with Inspector Johnston. "Just say you didn't know that it was even in there," I said.

So, next morning, my father called the number and, as he later told me, after a few minutes was put through to Inspector Johnston. After a few pleasantries, and they were few, my father told me later, the inspector asked my father if he was aware of the reason he wished to speak with him. My father said yes. He said that I had told him that the police claimed that an illegal gaming machine was in the licensed premises. The inspector said that he was correct, but neither he nor my father mentioned its disappearance.

The inspector asked my father if he was aware of the gaming machine being on the premises. My father replied that he was not as, while he was the licence holder, he left matters

74

to Mr. Martin. He added, "Mr. Martin is the man we have running the bar for us."

"Yes," said the inspector. "We know Mr. Martin runs the premises, but if charges are to be brought, and it is likely they will be, it will be you who will be named on the summons and brought to court, as you are the licence holder. I presume you have a solicitor in Northern Ireland?"

My father just said, "Yes, I do", naming his solicitor, who had an office in Derry.

"So, Mr. McGurk, you will be informed in due course if a prosecution is to be brought," he said. End of conversation.

And so, no surprise, about a month later, the brown envelope dropped through my father's letterbox, as did a similar one to his solicitor's office in Derry, stating that *Leo McGurk, Carrigans, Co. Donegal*, was to be *prosecuted under the Betting, Gaming and Lotteries Act*, etc., etc. and that *he and/or his legal representative*, was to appear in court, in Coleraine, on a specified date.

My father decided not to go, but to leave matters in the hands of his solicitor. His solicitor advised him that there was the danger of being questioned under oath. He couldn't lie, but an admission of knowingly allowing the machine to be in the premises wouldn't go down too well either. The solicitor suggested that I go in his place. He, the solicitor, would enter a 'guilty' plea and claim ignorance on my father's part as to the existence of the machine, throwing ourselves at the mercy of the judge and hoping for some mitigation on the basis that my father seldom visited the bar and wasn't well up on the gaming act (or whatever law he was accused of breaking) and this was his first offence. The reason the solicitor advised that I should go was that, should neither of us make an appearance, it could look like we were snubbing the court. So I agreed to attend. Once he entered a guilty plea, he said, we would hopefully get off with a light fine.

And so the day of the court came and both my father's solicitor and I attended. Kevin Boucher got a summons as well, but during the short hearing, he was not called. When the case did come up, there began some discussion between the judge, Inspector Johnston and our solicitor, plus another wig who I presumed was the QC for the Crown. I couldn't make out the exact words as the acoustics in the courtroom were not good and they were talking quietly among themselves. But I got the gist of it, and that was that our solicitor was pleading for a let off, or a small fine, on the basis that it was a first offence.

"Mr. McGurk," he added, "has held the licence for almost twenty-five years, without blemish."

The inspector then whispered something to the QC, but I saw the judge shake his head.

"Mr. McGurk junior is not the licence holder, nor has he been charged with any offence, and I am not comfortable with him being questioned when his father is not present," said the judge.

I was greatly relieved.

But Inspector Johnston countered that not only had there been a gaming machine on the premises on the day in question – he and a fellow officer had both seen it – but when the police returned to seize the machine, it had been taken away by person or persons unknown. The inspector added that, if the machine had not been removed in an attempt to frustrate the law, the seizure of the machine and the cash therein would have probably sufficed, and it was likely that no further charges would have been brought.

Aye and if you believe that, you'd believe anything, I thought to myself.

So, to cut a long story short, the judge took this removal of the machine into account, and he brooked no plea for mitigation and fined my father two hundred and fifty pounds. A hefty fine. Of course at that stage the fine wasn't heavy because of the *presence* of the poker machine, it was because of the *absence* of it, when the heavy squad arrived to lift it.

To put it simply, they hit us hard, not for having a poker machine, but for making eejits of them.

At the conclusion, we stepped out of court and the solicitor said to me that, given the circumstances, it wasn't too bad. It could have been much worse. My father could have had an endorsement on his licence or even lost it. Just then, another solicitor tapped our solicitor on the shoulder and for a few moments he was distracted.

At that same moment, Inspector Johnston appeared at my side and nodded at me to accompany him for a short distance. When we were out of earshot, he said, "Okay, I suppose you could say we both won and at the same time we both lost. You got away with it – this time."

His tone was quite informal. He was almost smiling and he had his hat in his hand. I wondered how he came to the conclusion that we 'got away with it', seeing as my father had just been fined two hundred and fifty pounds. But I said nothing.

"Tell me, just out of curiosity. What would you have said if you had been put in the box?"

"Dunno," I said, shrugging my shoulders. "Depends what I would have been asked."

The less said, the better, I thought.

"Well anyway," he said, "the case is over now and there's nothing personal. We have a job to do. But I want to just ask you this before I go…I know the machine was in the pub earlier. I know it and you know it. I saw it. Sergeant Crawford saw it. I even put a couple of fifty-pence pieces into it, while I was there. So I'm curious as to what you did with it. Where *did* you hide it? In the fishermen's little house?"

Just at that moment, before I answered, who appeared from the group of police officers, who were standing about, only Sourpuss herself, in full uniform, cap and all, but this time her hair was tied up behind her head. She approached us and tapped the Inspector on the shoulder. She actually looked very attractive in her uniform, so just to wind her up, when the Inspector turned round, I gave her one of my best smiles. She wasn't in the least amused. I was standing half behind the Inspector as he had turned around to face her, so he didn't see me smiling at her.

"Can I have a word, Inspector?" she said, looking at her superior officer, as she tried to hide her anger.

"Not now, can you give us a moment, please," the Inspector replied, which made her even more livid. He didn't want to be interrupted as he endeavoured to find out from me who had put me wise to the imminent raid at the Point.

She turned to leave but not without giving me another one of her looks. Remember I said that last time we met she gave me one of the foulest looks anyone could give, well, that one was in the ha'penny place compared to the one she give me this time. So just to put the icing on the cake, I winked at her as I smiled. I thought she was going to burst a blood vessel, there and then. The case was over and she couldn't arrest me for winking, so I just didn't care.

But Inspector Johnston saw me smiling at her. He glanced back at his sergeant, as she walked away, then turned back to me. Something was going through his mind. With a slightly puzzled look, he said to me, as he pointed his thumb over his shoulder, "Do you know Sergeant Crawford? Have you met her before?"

"No," I answered. "The only time I met her, apart from today, was the day you both came to the Point in plain clothes."

He pondered for a moment, then said, "Well anyway, you were saying…about the poker machine. Where did you hide it? In the small fishermen's house?"

I said, "No actually, Inspector, I wasn't saying anything about hiding it, before your sergeant appeared. But you know what, I will tell you now. Yes, we removed it, but we didn't put it in the fisherman's hut. We put it into the back of my van. I hoped you wouldn't think of the van."

He smiled. "Ah the van, very clever, very clever indeed. I'll give you ten out of ten for that one." He half turned to walk away then stopped. And I just knew why and what was coming next.

"Sorry, Frank, just one more thing, just between ourselves." He was back in the smiley mode. "We know that you got a tip-off. So, who gave it to you? Who phoned you?"

I looked at him. This was the real question. He wanted to know who the canary was. Who blew the whistle? I dropped my voice and said to him, "Nobody tipped me off, Inspector. I'll tell you how I knew."

I paused for a moment and then looked around to make sure no-one was within earshot.

I moved a step closer to him and spoke as quietly as I could.

"The word was going round for a week or more that the police were clamping down on poker machines and were lifting them in a big green van. Everyone knew it. So that day, purely by coincidence, I was up in the sand dunes behind the fishermen's hut, loosening a button, as they say, for a call of nature, when I saw, far away, just passing the prison, the big green van coming down the road. So I pulled up my trousers from around my ankles, held them up as best I could and ran like hell to the bar, shouted for a few of the boys to come quickly. We lifted the poker machine and pushed it into the van and drove it around the side, just before the green van pulled in."

The inspector looked at me. Putting on his hat, he said, "Yes, I'm sure that's what you did. You ran, carried out the gaming machine, opened the van, put the machine in and closed the van, all the while holding your trousers up. Took some doing!"

He walked off, but after two steps he turned, smiled and said, as he adjusted his hat on his head, "We'll meet again, Mr. McGurk." He was none too pleased, I suppose.

However, I never saw either Inspector Ian Johnston, or Sergeant whatever-her-first-name-was Crawford after that day outside court in Coleraine.

I heard later that the word was out that Inspector Johnston and his good-looking sergeant were both the butt of some slagging back in their station.

The story became legendary and was talked about for years afterwards. Even policemen who I knew were aware of the 'sting'. I gathered from the general gossip, that neither Inspector Johnston nor Sourpuss got any sympathy from the police in Limavady. Most of the cops in Limavady knew John and Marie Martin and they didn't take kindly to officers from a different district, stepping on their patch. Whatever the reason.

I said above that I never saw either Inspector Ian Johnston, or Sergeant Crawford after that day in Coleraine…but that was not strictly true.

About twenty years later, twenty-one to be exact, my wife and I were dining with another couple in a well-known Chinese restaurant in Coleraine. About halfway through our meal, I got up to go to the gents. I passed a man sitting at a table and we exchanged nods. I just nodded, because he nodded at me, but I didn't recognise him. His face didn't ring a bell.

As I was coming back from the men's room, he stood up and put out his hand.

"Mr. McGurk, isn't it?" he said. We shook hands.

The moment he spoke, it was the voice that did it for me. I might forget a face, but I never forget a voice. My memory cells were going at a million miles per hour, trying to figure out who he was. I knew that it had to be something to do with Magilligan and then, *Eureka!*

I had him. It was none other than my 'old friend', Inspector Ian Johnston.

"Hello, Mr. McGurk. Long time," he said as we shook.

"Yes, Frank McGurk…and you're Inspector Johnston," I said.

"Yes," he replied. "But retired, long retired."

"Small world, Inspector," I said.

"Ian," he said. "Just call me Ian."

He laughed but I felt at the time that it was not a genuine laugh.

"It's been a long time, Frank. What, fifteen, twenty years?"

"It will be twenty-one years, come this summer," I said.

"You're not serious," he said, in mock disbelief.

I was dying to ask him about Sourpuss, but decided against it. She would be an old bag by now, anyway, I thought to myself! He looked down at his partner, turned back to me and said, "Frank, this is my wife, Dorothy."

We exchanged smiles.

We broke handshake, as he turned to his wife again and said, "Dorothy, remember I told you many times about the lad who said he was loosening a button in the sand hills at Magilligan, yet managed to run to the pub and remove a poker machine – with his trousers half on and half off? Well, this is he. This is the very man himself!"

He was smiling as he said this.

His wife began to laugh, but her mouth was full, so after a moment she finished her bite, set down her knife and fork, wiped her mouth with her napkin and looked up at me.

"You know, Frank, Ian has told that story many times," she said. "I wish I had a pound for every time I heard it. He practically dined out on that one."

"Well, well, there you go now. Doesn't time fly," he repeated. "Do you still own the pub?"

I said that we didn't. We had sold it on to a local man, Seamus McLaughlin, some years ago.

"Oh yes, of course. I knew Seamus from his days in Ballymaclary House," he said.

After a few pleasantries, the conversation dried up, so we shook hands and I said goodbye to him and his wife and turned to go.

As I did so, he touched me on the arm and said quietly, "So, are you going to tell me, Frank? Just for old times' sake, as they say. We all knew you got a tip-off. But, sure now that it's practically ancient history, go on, tell me. Who *did* tip you off? Sure, it doesn't matter now, I'm retired anyhow."

Aye, I thought to myself. *Retired? …you boys never retire.*

I looked at him, paused for a moment, his wife had even stopped chewing. And then I looked around the restaurant, bent forward a little towards him. He put his ear closer in expectation, and I then said, almost in a whisper, "It happened like this. I was loosening a button in the sand hills, for a call of nature, when I saw…"

"Ah, Jesus, not that old bull again." he said as he slapped me on the shoulder. "I should have known better than to ask you."

Still smiling, we shook hands again and he sat down. I turned and walked back to my table, sat down and continued with my meal. As I sat there, I thought about the whole episode again and suddenly I had a thought. It might have been over twenty years ago, but I didn't forget his efforts to persuade the judge to come down hard on us.

Or the scowl old Sourpuss gave me – and I was only trying to be nice to her!

Within a minute, I knew exactly what I was going to do.

I kept an eye on them and when they got up and made their way to the till, I too got up from my seat and made for the toilets, again. As I passed them at the till, I stopped and tapped him on the shoulder. He turned around and was a little surprised to see that it was me again.

I spoke quietly to him.

"You were right all along, Inspector. I did get a tip-off, on the telephone, about half an hour before you arrived back."

He didn't correct my naming him 'Inspector'.

"Go on," he said, as he pretended to go through his bill. He didn't look at me but continued to examine the till receipt. For that fleeting moment, he had his inspector's hat back on, metaphorically speaking.

"Just between you and me now," says I. "It was a lady who called, about half an hour before you arrived back. All she said was that our poker machine was about to be seized. Then she hung up. That's all I know. Obviously, she didn't leave her name, but I do remember one thing."

"What's that?" he asked, without lifting his head. By this time, his wife had turned and was listening to the conversation with much curiosity. I made sure both of them heard what I was going to say.

"She spoke with an English accent. Just like your one, the actress, Joanna Lumley, you know who I mean?"

He looked at me straight in the eye and his smile disappeared.

His face practically turned scarlet and his wife gave him a real angry look. I knew, just then, that I had hit the bullseye – dead centre. He was about to say something, but his wife had already made for the door and he turned to catch up with her. I turned and walked into the toilet. I stayed there a short while and when I emerged, both he and his wife had gone.

It might have taken nearly twenty-one years, but it was worth the wait.

I felt as if I'd just dealt the old inspector a hand of aces and eights and all black!

*some names have been changed.

3

Twelve O'Clock High

Four men head out duck shooting on the river in a dodgy boat. Will it get them back to shore?

Gun	*Check*
Cartridge belt	*Check*
Ammo	*Check*
Game bag	*Check*
Duck caller	*Check*
Hat	*Check*
Big coat	*Check*
Torch	*Check*
Flask	*Check*
Sandwiches	*Check*
Engine	*Check*
Spare petrol	*Check*
Bailing pan	*Check*

You had to make sure you had everything, so I had a habit of writing it all down the day before and then, on the morning of the big day, 1st September, it was all checked off, to make sure we didn't forget anything. Just like a dawn patrol in Kabul.

But this was no Kabul, we were going duck shooting and luckily, unlike the Taliban, the ducks didn't shoot back.

This was what we called the 'opening morning', that is, the opening day of the shooting season, when you could legally shoot duck and other wildfowl.

Different game have different dates and seasons when they can be legally hunted. The earliest in the year is the shooting of grouse, which opens on 12th August, long known as the Glorious Twelfth, but there weren't too many grouse in our locality and it was a heavy walk through thick heather, where they are normally found. So I think from memory, I only went grouse shooting once or twice.

Next on the shooting calendar is 1st September when, as I have said, is the season when duck can be legally shot, and also certain breeds of geese. The geese season only lasts a couple of weeks, whereas you can shoot duck until 31st January. 1st November opens the pheasant season.

All shooting stops on 31st January, so from 1st February until 1st September, it is ceasefire season.

Which meant that by 1st September we were itching to get back out shooting again. For a week beforehand, we would check the tides on the river to see what stage they would be on the opening morning. Would it be high tide, low tide, ebbing tide or flooding tide? Would it be spring tides or neap tides? All these factors you had to take into account when planning the big morning.

Normally our destination was an area of reed beds situated in the River Foyle at St. Johnston in Donegal. This area of reeds was, and of course still is, called the Hollocks. The Hollocks were not exactly in the middle of the river, being nearer to the Donegal side than to the far side, which is

County Tyrone. The River Foyle at St. Johnston is almost a mile wide.

The Hollocks are about three acres in size and, as I say, consist of an area of raised reed beds. It is a favourite place for mallard and teal to fly into, especially during the morning and dusk flight from the fields.

On 1st September, dawn strikes about 5.30 a.m., but duck will be on the wing earlier – from about 5 a.m. They are flying back to the reeds, after spending the night in fields, feeding. Now, while our intention is to stay out for three or four hours, in actual fact the first and best flight can be as short as ten or fifteen minutes. Then it's over. What duck you get after that are a few latecomers, or scared ducks flying from one refuge to another.

But, of course, duck don't just stop flying after the first flight, as solitary or pairs of duck will always be on the wing somewhere on the river. Perhaps they have been shot at away upriver and have been scared down to the Hollocks. A few shots there and, if they have escaped that hail of buckshot, they fly on to the next place of relative safety. If there are many sportsmen out, there are fewer places for the duck to go and so there are always a few on the wing.

Of course, that's only on the opening morning. After that morning, the ducks get some degree of peace.

The blitzkrieg eases off.

So, on the morning I'm talking about, which would have been in the mid nineteen eighties, we calculated that high tide was between 2 a.m. and 3 a.m.

At 5 a.m. or 5.30 a.m., the time when we would begin our voyage across to the Hollocks from the shore, the tide was still too high to walk out to the Hollocks, so a boat was required.

The shortest distance to the Hollocks was from a place called Rankin's Shore, so we had to get a boat a day beforehand, get it to Rankin's Shore, tie it up and hide it, and it would be there for us in the early morning. And if we needed a boat, Scobie was our man.

Scobie, whose real name was John Duddy, always kept a decent boat at the old quay in St. Johnston, locally known as the Boathole. He had often allowed us to borrow his boat in previous years. So Wilbert and I went to Scobie the day before the opening morning and, as we had done on previous occasions, asked him if we could borrow his boat for the next morning. But unfortunately, we had left it too late and Scobie had already promised it to someone else.

However, all was not lost. He had a second boat which he offered us – not as big or as robust as the one he usually loaned us, but we had little choice but to avail of it. We had no other option if we wanted to get out to the Hollocks. It lay up on the bank and he was right, it looked a poor specimen compared to his better boat. But beggars can't be choosers, so we accepted his offer.

So Wilbert and I thanked Scobie and managed to drag the boat into the burn. The tide was falling rapidly, so we had to get it down to Rankin's Shore as quickly as possible, or we would be grounded. But the ebbing tide was in our favour and with little effort from the oars and only two of us in the boat, we reached Rankin's Shore in no time. Stepping out of the boat, we hid it deep in the bushes, tied it up and headed home.

We didn't really need to hide it, as strangely enough there was always an unwritten law which was that no-one ever stole a boat. Well, that's the way it was in the old days.

Having the boat here at Rankin's Shore would make life a lot easier the following morning. It would be a simple and short run across to the Hollocks, courtesy of a 4hp engine, which Wilbert, James and I owned between us. You could say it was a company engine!

As I say, it all depended on timing and movement of the tides. Too high a tide, then you needed a boat and engine, or oars, as it was too deep to wade through. Too low a tide and you ran the chance of the boat not having enough water to float, so you're stuck, literally. The return to Rankin's Shore after the couple of hours shooting had to be taken into account also, as the same perils applied. The last thing you wanted was to be stuck in mud, out there in the Hollocks, all day, until the next high tide came to float a boat off.

Having tied the boat up securely and hidden the oars, Wilbert and I said our goodbyes and went home, eagerly awaiting the coming dawn. Now, Scobie's boat was good enough for two people, dodgy with three, but really not suitable for any more. But there were only three of us anyway, so we should be okay. Or so I thought.

I was no sooner home when Paddy Doherty arrived at the door. Paddy was better known as the Blue Jesus, or Paddy Blue Jesus.

"Are yc going out to the ducks in the morning?" he asks.

"Aye, we are," says I.

"Where are yez going to?" he asks. And he told him we were going to the Hollocks.

"I might get a run out with ye," he says, inviting himself.

Paddy worked for us on a regular, if not permanent basis and I didn't like to refuse. So rightly or wrongly I agreed to take him along and told him to be at our house at a quarter to five the next morning – sharp.

"I'll be there," says Paddy.

So that night, I loaded everything except for my gun, waders and coat into the van, and after watching a bit of television, I turned in at about 10 p.m., having set the clock for 4.30 a.m.

It only seemed like ten minutes later when the alarm in my bedside clock rang and I hopped out of bed. I was only half asleep anyway so I knew it was almost time to rise. You never slept well that night anyway. At last, the long-awaited opening morning had arrived. After dressing, I toasted a few slices of bread, buttered and jammed them, before wrapping them in kitchen foil and placing them in a small Tupperware container. The kettle was boiled and a flask of tea made. I scrounged through the biscuit box, found a half packet of chocolate digestives, and together the flask of tea, the toast and the biscuits were duly set into the game bag. I put on my waders, looked around to make sure I hadn't forgotten anything, lifted the bag and my gun and unlocked the back door. I locked it again behind me and opened the van door. My checklist was lying there, so I took one last glance at it, saw that it was okay and got into the van.

There wasn't a sound.

At exactly 4.45 a.m., Paddy pulls into the yard and parks up.

"Are we going in your van?" he asks.

"Aye," says I. "Get in."

So Paddy, similarly attired with waders and gun, game bag and cartridges, got into the van. Now Paddy was a connoisseur of the 'F' and 'B' words and, while I'll try to keep

92

these to a minimum, the story wouldn't be the same without Paddy's liberal use in his vocabulary.

"Where are we going?" was the first thing he asked.

"Rankin's Shore," I replied. "We have a boat of Scobie's hidden there."

"Grand," he says.

We headed through Carrigans and in a couple of minutes or less we were parked at the head of Rankin's Lane, from where a short walk of about a hundred yards would take us to the water's edge.

It was still pitch dark.

Within a few minutes, Wilbert and James arrived and pulled in beside my van. I told them quietly that Paddy Blue Jesus had inveigled himself into the shooting party, but they didn't mind. Wilbert did remark to me quietly that four in Scobie's boat, plus the engine, might be dodgy. But nothing more was said, and having divided all the gear between Wilbert, James and Paddy, I carried the outboard engine over my shoulder.

From here on, all the conversation became whispers, although I don't believe it made any difference. No ducks were listening to us anyway. It was all just part of the ritual.

"Has somebody got the petrol jar?" James asked.

"Aye," says Paddy. "I have it."

We walked down the lane, making as little noise as we could. Away somewhere in the hills across in Tyrone, a tractor could be heard turning over, before its engine throbbed into life. The sound carried easily across the calm water.

"Somebody's up early," says I.

"Sounds like a big yawk," says Paddy.

"That's a John Deere," says Wilbert, giving us the benefit of his knowledge of tractors.

"Ah, you wouldn't know the difference between a John Deere and a Dear John," said James.

But Wilbert didn't bite and on we walked. Soon, after scaling two gates, we arrived at the shore.

Now at this stage, while I have said that the intended destination was the Hollocks, it wasn't just anywhere in the mass of reed beds that made up the Hollocks; it was very important to get to the two main clumps of reeds, which were at the downstream end. This is the place that we called the 'point' of the Hollocks. Get in there and you got first shot at any duck coming from away down in the lough, from where they would undoubtedly be scared away once the firing started down there.

So it was vital to get to the front. If someone else got there before you, you were playing a serious second fiddle and your chances of a first shot were scuppered.

So as not to let anyone beat us to the point of the Hollocks, we kept as quiet as we could, extracted the boat from where we had hidden it, and while the other boys set the bags and other bits and bobs into the boat, I mounted the outboard engine on the back board of the boat and tightened the wing nuts to keep it in place.

But when doing so, I noticed that the back board was somewhat loose and the weight of the engine and thrust of the propeller would widen the gap as it pushed the boat forward.

I told myself that I needed to keep an eye on it.

When we were all set to go, I told the other three to get in and I gave the boat a push into somewhat deeper water and climbed aboard. On the second pull of the engine, it roared into life. There was no point in being quiet then, it was a dash to the point. The three boys were in front of me, I was operating the outboard so, knocking the gear lever into forward, we headed across the deep to our intended spot. James and Wilbert sat on the one seat, while Paddy sat at the bow. The boat settled lower than I liked in the water, which worried me a bit, and the water was coming in through the gap, but I said nothing.

Of course, we hadn't a life jacket between us. But who needs life jackets? Sure isn't the dry land just over there! We never even thought about life jackets in those days.

In the distance we could hear another outboard. We thought it might be Sox. The old fox would be making for the same spot as us. But we got to the front reed beds before him with a bit of good luck, and we left Wilbert and Paddy off on top of the first bed, while James and I continued to the second of the two beds.

And just in time. As we pulled in, Brendan Devine, or Sox as he was better known, along with someone else who we didn't recognise in the dark, pulled in just after us.

We had beaten him to the draw. Just.

It was an understood thing that the first hunters to get there got exclusive rights to stay, and anyway, too many guns at the one spot was somewhat dangerous. So after a bit of banter, Sox and his sidekick moved off and headed across to where Paddy and Wilbert were concealed. He didn't know they were there, and we didn't tell him. But he should have seen the occasional glow of Paddy's eternal cigarette. So after the short crossing, Sox pulled into the reed bed, where Wilbert and Paddy were and began getting himself squared up.

In the dark, we heard Paddy. We just knew what was coming next.

"Fuck off, Sox, get yer ain place," says Paddy.

You could have heard him in Lifford.

So Sox and his shooting partner turned around and made for a spot in the centre of the Hollocks. Not the worst spot, but not as good as ours.

James and I then got our guns loaded up, a box of extra cartridges opened and at the ready, and I put the duck caller in my mouth and blew a short couple of quacks, just to see if a lonely drake somewhere needed company. No reply. Nothing on the wing yet. Nothing that we could hear anyhow. It was still pitch dark, but the funny thing is you got used to it and you could see much more than you would think.

At this stage, James said to me, "Did you see the back of the boat, when we were crossing?"

"I did," says I.

"Too many in the boat," says James.

"I know. But I couldn't refuse Paddy when he asked me last night. I didn't know the back board was so loose until I mounted the engine at Rankin's Shore."

James had also noticed the continuous inflow of water, and after a better examination I could see that the stern board was actually coming loose, and the counter force of the outboard made the situation worse. I had had to slacken the speed and physically hold the board closed on the way across from the shore. When we had parted company with Wilbert and Paddy and pulled into our own bed of reeds, I managed to find some twine lying in the boat, which I used to sweel[*]

---

[*]**Sweel…***Ulster/Scots, to wrap tightly, swaddle.*

around the rear board and a part of the side of the boat. A couple of knots and it seemed firm enough.

"What do you think?" says James.

"Well, it should be okay now. And I think by the time we're ready to leave the tide will be low enough for us to get back safely," I ventured. "It should hold until we get back across."

"Hope so," says James.

From the reeds to the shore was not too far, maybe a hundred yards or a bit more. But the tricky bit was, although relatively shallow between the Hollocks and the shore, there was a deep channel which ran all the way down, not far out from the shore and not too wide, but much too deep to walk through. This deep channel flowed between the shore and the Hollocks. The trick is knowing where exactly it was when the tide was medium high.

"We'll be okay. The tide will be well dropped," I said quietly.

"I suppose so," says James, "but we'll say nothing. There's no point in frightening everyone."

"Agreed," says I.

Soon, conversation ceased and we waited...and waited...and waited.

Somewhere up about the islands, a shot went off. But still we couldn't see or hear any duck. I blew another long quack and a couple of short ones into the caller.

Still no response.

Now James and I had worked out a directional plan some years before, which, although looked very much like we were playing at *The Dam Busters* or *633 Squadron*, was, despite sounding a bit naff, very effective. We picked out one point downriver right ahead of us, say a very bright streetlight in Bready which was maybe ten miles away. We called that twelve o'clock, and everything in the three hundred and sixty degrees around us became a clock face. So, facing the bright light, six o'clock was directly behind us, three o'clock was ninety degrees to the right, and nine o'clock, ninety degrees to our left.

When one of us spied a duck or flock of duck, instead of saying, "Over there, near the barley field" or "over that farm shed roof", trying to describe from which direction the duck or pair of ducks were approaching, we just said "two o'clock" or "five o'clock" and we immediately knew from what direction the ducks were approaching. We would sit back-to-back with me covering everything from three o'clock to nine o'clock while James covered nine o'clock to three. Every angle was covered. All we had to do now is wait.

And if the duck was flying from the bright light direction and was high in the sky, then it was "twelve o'clock high" and if it was approaching low, just above the water, it was simply "twelve o'clock low."

Guy Gibson couldn't have planned it better.

A peewit called somewhere and, far away, we heard the cry of a curlew.

It's funny, I had often heard the dawn chorus in springtime and it is a truly magical experience to hear the multitude of birds, all singing their own melodious song, as they welcome the rising spring sun. My mother, God bless her, used to talk about it every year, often asking me if I had heard the dawn chorus that morning. Of course, I didn't when I was young. Who wakens at dawn when you're young? As I got older, I did hear it occasionally. But my mother never failed to hear it, every year.

In fact she went through her final minutes on this earth, as the May dawn chorus was at its loudest. I think every bird in the firmament, it sounded like, had put in a special effort for her, on her last morning.

But what I'm certain of is that my mother never experienced being in the Hollocks on a September morning, listening to the autumn dawn chorus. That dawn chorus was made up of all sorts of wading birds, waterfowl and the many other species of birds that graced the shore, especially when the tide was out and they could forage for all sorts of tiny marine creatures that emerged with the recession of the tide. The sound would carry for miles, and it is truly wondrous to behold. You can hear lapwings, sometimes called peewits, from their call, the curlew and the plover. Perhaps a pair of swans will bid you good morning with a couple of honks, as they make for mid river, after spending the night in the nearby fields.

As we sit there, not a word is spoken. We are in complete sound lockdown.

While we hear all these different sounds, the experienced hunter will immediately pick out the chatter of a faraway drake as he paddles among the reeds, or the beat of the wings of a teal, flying overhead in the dark. It is as beautiful a chorus as the spring one. But sadly, it doesn't get the same popular coverage.

But you know that it will be broken by the *bang-bang* of a hunter's double barrel, somewhere upriver, or maybe far away downriver. It could be a genuine hunter firing at a duck, or it could be a novice who can't wait and fires blindly at the sound of a beating wing overhead.

We were on full alert by now, knowing that it was only minutes until the war started. All was quiet and we had our eyes peeled and still we waited…and waited. As it began to slowly clear, we could see that Wilbert and Paddy were actually closer to us than had seemed in the dark. We could now see a bird in the sky – it had cleared enough.

"See anything?" I spoke softly to them.

"Nope," was the reply.

"The bright light is twelve o'clock," I said to them, pointing downriver. Wilbert understood and gave me the thumbs-up.

He had also seen *The Dam Busters*. But he told us afterwards that Paddy didn't understand and asked, "What the fuck is he *twelve o'clocking* about? Sure it's not even six o'clock!"

James then said to me quietly, "Do you think the boat will be okay to take us in?"

"Aye, sure we have the bailing pan, anyway," says I.

"Aye, of course, the bailing pan," said James. "That should keep us okay."

"Don't worry," says I. "The tide…"

I never got to finish the sentence, as James ducked down suddenly and swung his gun to the right.

"Two o'clock low…two o'clock low," he says, and I swivelled round also.

Two mallard were winging their way towards us and their landing gear was down.

"Hold...hold...hold," I whispered, pushing the safety catch forward. We held back until they were directly overhead.

"Now," I called and both of us fired at them directly above us. But they were too close and we missed both. One wheeled away to the west, while the other, in an attempt to fly on, hit a fusillade from Wilbert or Paddy and fell dead in the mud beside them.

Suddenly, it was like Okinawa, shooting everywhere. The dawn flight had begun. This was the short period when our clock routine was no use. There were ducks coming and going from twelve o'clock to six o'clock – and back to twelve. Paddy must have been totally confused at what was going on, hearing all this.

"Two o'clock low." *Bang-bang!*

"Six o'clock high." *Bang-bang!*

Then as suddenly as it began, it seemed, it was over. The best of it, anyway. Although it seemed short, it had lasted the best part of ten minutes. And also, in that short space of time, it had suddenly become daylight.

It was all quiet again, punctured by occasional shots from far up at the islands or maybe at Tony's Gut, or away downriver below Hanna's Point. I refilled my cartridge belt, checked the open box lying on the reed bed and opened another box beside it.

We tallied up, three mallard and two teal – not a great bag for the dawn flight, but we weren't finished yet. Wilbert and Paddy had bagged four mallard, but I suspect Wilbert had shot most of them.

Now was the time when the point of the Hollocks was the best place to be. It was the first port of call for a solitary duck, or pair of ducks, perhaps seeking sanctuary from another Okinawa, away downriver.

There was another dead drake floating down past us out in the main stream and we debated whether to row out to get it. But when I lowered the oar upright into the water, it went down almost four feet, and it would be deeper out where the duck was, so we abandoned the idea, given that our boat was somewhat like *Titanic.* The back end was breaking loose – and we had no lifeboats. They hadn't enough on *Titanic* either. But we had a bailing pan which could discharge as much, if not more, water out as was coming in.

So, we were on the right side of the mathematics, unlike poor old Captain Smith, who didn't even have a bailing pan! Not that it would have done him much good.

So we bailed a bit, sat a bit and waited a bit…

As we concluded that the next attack would not come for several minutes, we dipped into our bags and extracted the goodies. James had sandwiches, which certainly looked like they were not made by him, but by his good wife, Heather. He also had, what I called two Presbyterian buns, i.e. beautiful little traybakes, freshly made. He didn't have a hand in baking these either. James' culinary talents were, I suspect, a bit like my own. I soon had the two slices of toast eaten and after giving James a bogus "twelve o'clock, low," which momentarily distracted him, I relieved him of his second Presbyterian bun, resulting in a half whispered, "You thieving bastard!"

However, a handful of chocolate digestives bought the peace.

It's funny, but there was always something very tasty about a flask of tea and a sandwich or two, when you're out shooting early in the morning – and a Presbyterian bun!

Five minutes later there wasn't a crumb left, so we packed up the flasks and the Tupperware sandwich boxes and got back on sentinel duty.

I tested the oar in the water again and the tide had dropped a fair bit from last time. Now, as I have alluded to, the tide had to be timed perfectly. The one thing you had to avoid at all costs, was letting the tide go too low before you headed back to shore. If it got too low, there was a big risk of the boat getting stuck on the bottom and you had to drag it through the glar[*]– an almost impossible task, as your waders were getting stuck at every step. So, while we kept a watch for ducks, we had to be conscious of the water level. A solitary duck flew high between our two reed beds, but I didn't give any of the others the warning and I got the first shot in and hit it. A split second later, Paddy fired and we could see a few feathers coming off. But by that stage, it was dead.

So I said to Paddy, "Why did you do that, Paddy?"

"Do what?" he asked, somewhat puzzled, as if he had done something wrong.

"Shoot a dead duck," I said, with a serious voice.

"What do you mean, *shoot a dead duck*?" Paddy asks.

"Well," says I, without the slightest hint of sarcasm, "by the time you fired at that one, Paddy, I had the duck shot, plucked and oven ready! You were too slow. You were shooting dead ones!"

---

[*]**glar**…*Scots/Irish, thick sticky mud, found in river estuaries.*

Paddy didn't answer, but looked the other way, shaking his head. He was not amused.

We stayed another twenty minutes or so, but we only added one duck to the bag, courtesy of a lucky snapshot by James. Wilbert and Paddy looked across at us and we knew what we were all thinking. Time to go. So, as it was too shallow for the engine and too deep to wade, we got out the oars. I unscrewed the thumb bolts of the engine and lifted it into the boat. We wouldn't need it again.

James got down on the seat, facing backwards of course, fitted the oars into the rollocks, or as they are properly called, row locks, and he began to pull slowly. Paddy and Wilbert gathered up their gear and waited for us to arrive over. But James efforts at rowing were not of the Oxford–Cambridge quality and he nearly hit me a couple of times with an oar.

Eventually, after going this way and that, James managed to get the boat manoeuvred alongside Wilbert and Paddy, who stepped in, and Paddy volunteered to do the rowing. He was used to this from his fishing days. James agreed, crossed the oars on the sides of the boat, stood up and was glad to let Paddy at it.

So Paddy sits down, extends the oars, while James goes to the front of the boat, where he helps balance the boat.

He and Wilbert sat at the front, myself plus the engine at the back, and Paddy Blue Jesus in the middle. But while we were evenly balanced, it was obvious that we were overloaded, and the boat sat very low in the water. It was much the same on the way out, but it had been pitch dark and no-one had noticed. Although I suppose we each had a fair idea but said nothing.

James and Wilbert and I were familiar with the river, and we knew that despite looking ominous, we were in fact in relatively shallow water and the only problem left was to get across the small, yet deep, channel. Once across that, we knew that we were home and dry. Of course, because the water was completely muddy, if you didn't know the score regarding the true depth, you wouldn't know whether you were in two feet of water or twenty-two feet. But I knew it was quite deep beside the reed beds. From there it was comparatively shallow right to the shore, except for the one deep channel, which was close to the shore. So, before Paddy got into action, I dipped an oar vertically into the water beside the reed bed and it went down to the handle. I could see Paddy looking at it with some apprehension, but of course, the moment we left the reed bed, the water depth came up to only about two feet.

With four of us in the boat, the situation was still dodgy, because if the boat did sink, we weren't in very deep water, but we still had to get across the channel. Paddy, however, was not aware of the shallowness of the water, nor did he know about the deep channel. He assumed it was deep all the way from the reed beds we had just left to the shore.

The water was rising in the boat. The twine holding the back board had become loose and water was flowing in rapidly. I shouted to James to start bailing as fast as he could. Behind Paddy's back, he began to bail. Wilbert lifted a stick that was lying in the boat and dipped it into the water. It just went about a foot down. Of course Paddy didn't see this as he was facing rearwards, but James and Wilbert and myself knew then that we were across the deep channel and that we were safe. But Paddy didn't know this and we didn't tell him. We knew we were in less than a foot of water.

"Pull, Paddy, pull faster," I called, in mock fear. "Pull like hell! We're sinking!"

Paddy rowed furiously.

"I'm pulling as fast as I fucking can!" he shouted.

"I know, Paddy. But we're sinking – fast! You need to pull faster."

"I'm pulling like the Blue Jesus," he gasped. "I can't row any fucking faster."

The sweat was running off him as he pulled his best. He could see the water pouring in through the crack at the back of the boat. While it looked as if we had still a good distance to go to reach the shore, it was in fact getting shallower with every yard and we expected the boat to ground at any moment.

Paddy called, "Jesus Christ, we're done, we're fucked."

"Oh, God save us," says James, as he bailed as fast as he could.

I then began to recite the Lord's prayer.

"Our Father, who art in Heaven, hallowed be thy name. Thy kingdom come."

As Paddy had his back to them, he couldn't see the two boyos splitting their sides but trying their best not to burst out laughing. Just then the boat came to a sudden stop. We had struck the bottom. Paddy couldn't understand for a moment how this could be. He stopped rowing.

I casually stepped out of the boat and said, "Hand me out those ducks there, Paddy."

Paddy stood up, looked at my legs and saw that the water barely reached my knees and then looked at Wilbert and James. They were still in stitches laughing. The sweat was pouring off Paddy and he was still panting.

The penny then dropped with him and he looked at us straight in the eye and says, "You bastards! You dirty rotten bastards."

"Aye," says James, trying to keep a straight face, "but we thought we were in deep water too. Jesus, Paddy, you saved our lives. You're a master oarsman. We'll have to put your name forward for the Olympic team."

"And a bravery medal," says Wilbert.

"Fuck off," says Paddy, and then muttered something which I didn't catch, as he made his way to the edge of the shore, just a few feet away. We left our gear on the ground. Paddy lit a much-needed cigarette and sat down on a stone, while Wilbert, James and I pushed and pulled the boat out of the water and managed to get it back up into a safe place, from which Wilbert and I retrieved it a few days later and returned it to Scobie. After, of course, hammering a few extra nails into the tailboard. Having gathered up our gear, we climbed over the gates and walked back up the lane and in no time we were back at our vehicles. During this time, Paddy didn't utter a single word and, given that Wilbert, James and I realised that perhaps we had gone a bit far with the practical joke, we didn't say much either.

We put all our own guns and bags into our respective vehicles, and I set the outboard engine into my van. James and Wilbert said their goodbyes. I reciprocated, but Paddy still didn't speak. We headed home.

Paddy didn't speak to me on the way home. He just took relief from another cigarette. When we got to my house, he got out of my van, put his gun and coat into the back of his van and reached for the handle of the driver's door.

As he opened it, he turned to me and said, "You might have thought that that carry-on was funny. But I didn't think it was funny. I thought we were goners. That's all I could think about, yet you all thought it was funny, making a right eejit of me."

"I'm sorry, Paddy," I said, as he climbed in. "We didn't mean to. It just was funny at the time."

He didn't answer me, but just drove off. But, while it took a long time, Paddy eventually could see the funny side of it.

Needless to say, the story often did the rounds in the local bars on many a night.

And if Paddy and I and some of my workmen were heading off to do a job and loading up the van with tools, someone was sure to say to Paddy, "Is the bailing pan in, Paddy?" or, "Have you the oars in, Paddy?"

The answer was always the same! With more than a few profanities to boot!

However, not long ago, before he passed away, Paddy and I met, and he told me that he had been given bad news by his doctor. He was seriously ill. Shortly after this, I went to visit Paddy and we talked about the old days, about the many ups and downs we encountered in the various jobs I had been involved in. We recounted the funny episodes and the not-so-funny and inevitably we recalled that famous shooting morning, many years ago. Thankfully, he had long ago got over his anger and we both laughed heartily about it.

Eventually, I got to my feet, and we shook hands as I left, but Paddy didn't make eye contact with me. We both knew the score. A couple of months later, Paddy went to his rest.

Paddy 'Blue Jesus' was a good man.

May he rest in peace.

4

Entente Cordiale

The body of a woman is found dead in a hedge.
But where is the hedge?

This story is not a long one. It doesn't have a happy beginning or ending and the bit in the middle isn't a bellyful of laughs either. But it is a true story nevertheless and I suppose similar events happen every day of the week. Just the names are different. But what makes this story unique is because of where it actually took place.

I remember hardly any of it, just the men in our kitchen drinking tea, but I managed to get bits and pieces of the story from my father in later years. In fact, not long before he went to his rest, on the long drive to Dublin one day, the subject came up again and he told me what he knew. I made a mental note of it and when I got home I scribbled what he told me down on a few pieces of paper. I didn't give it much thought in later years, until one day, not long ago, I discovered those papers in an old file. I thought they were lost long ago.

The story begins, in the clichéd way any story begins.

"The first I knew," my father said, "was when a knock came to the door, one dark winter's night, just before Christmas. About 1958, or maybe a year earlier."

He paused for a moment, and I said, "And what?"

I was driving. After a moment he started again. He was trying to remember the exact year, he said, but eventually he conceded that he couldn't remember which year it was. I was anxious to hear the story, so I told him to forget which year.

"Fifty-seven, fifty-eight, it doesn't matter," I said to him. Since then, I have tried to gather as much information as I can about the incident from the elderly neighbours who are still around. But no-one seems to know, or wants to talk about it. All I have managed to get were small bits and pieces from family members of those who have passed on. What my father told me was undoubtedly his memories, but he could only vouch for those parts, where he was personally involved. Some parts are, I suppose, what we would call hearsay. Questions still remain – questions that have never been satisfactorily answered and, I suppose now, never will.

At the time, we were living in a new house, which my father had built around 1955, quite close to the border between Northern Ireland and the Republic of Ireland, more commonly referred to then – and still – as the North and the South.

There was a knock at the door, he told me.

The front of our house faced on to a relatively minor country road. Beyond that road is a field and at the other side of that field the hedge forms the border between North and South. It is still called the Border Field and at the time it belonged to my father. It still belongs to our family.

A local farmer had the field 'taken', in other words rented (we ourselves weren't farmers), and as he was keeping cattle in it, he had erected a fence along and as close to the hedge as he could around the whole field.

The field was roughly rectangular and was bounded on the two short sides by a minor road at one end, and two gardens and houses at the other end. The farmer who owned the field next to it, on the Northern side, had his side fenced also.

The reason for two fences was quite simple and obvious–to prevent the cattle from wandering out of either field. The hedge wasn't just a narrow thorn hedge. It was actually a wall, built over years with surplus stones gathered from the field. Thorn bushes, whin and bramble and trees had, over many years, grown through the wall, practically leaving the stones invisible. But on its own the old wall and hedgerows would not have been good enough to keep the cattle in. Hence the two fences.

So, while there were and still are to this day two fences, one on each side of the hedge, the actual boundary between County Derry and County Donegal, and indeed the boundary between the North and the South would have been approximately in the middle between the two fences. But the lack of uniformity of the wall, plus the fences not being completely straight, meant that where the actual legal boundary was, or is, was not easy to figure out, if one needed to know. But there never was any real reason to determine the exact boundary line. An architect once told me that the width of a boundary line depends on the thickness of the pencil. In actual fact, he said, a boundary, unless specified how wide, is just a line.

Between the two fences, the bit in the middle was just a stone wall, covered, as I have stated, in all kinds of wild growth. A sort of no-man's-land you could say. The distance between the two fences would have been as narrow as two feet in some places, while at other places perhaps up to five feet wide. The farmer in the North had his side fenced, we had our side fenced – so who cared? Well, no-one really. Until that cold dark winter's night, almost sixty-five years ago.

When my father heard the knock, he opened the door and standing there was a neighbour, who he knew as Mickey McGlinchey. He was practically out of breath. My father knew Mickey, as most of us did, as he lived close to our house. Well, while I say 'lived', he was actually a Derry man, but for whatever reason he was lodging with a local family called Brown. Maggie Brown, the woman who owned the house, despite having a large family, occasionally took in lodgers.

Her house, like her neighbours the Ross family, had a garden, which I suppose many moons ago was part of our field, but were now attached to each house. Between each garden and our field was a single wire fence.

I never remember a Mr. Brown, but in those days and at that age, one didn't ask such questions. Mickey McGlinchey lodged there and that was that.

"Call the Guards," said Mickey to my father. "Quickly!"

Before doing so and possibly getting the Guards out on a wild goose chase, or perhaps a not-too-serious 'domestic', my father asked Mickey to give him a bit more detail. Very quickly, as Mickey blurted out his story, my father knew that Mickey wasn't imagining things and said that he would call the Guards immediately.

Mickey said he had to hurry home. So he left and my father closed the door and lifted the handset off the phone, which like most houses that had a telephone, sat on a small table in the hallway. To make a call, you turned the handle, which would, usually after a short delay, get you through to the local operator. In a short space of time, my father was

112

connected to the local Garda station. One solitary garda was on duty. The station sergeant lived not in the station, but close by.

Basically, the story Mickey had told my father and which he in turn relayed to the guard on the other end of the phone was this.

Mickey had gone out to gather kindling, a little earlier. Between Maggie's garden and our field, the fence had been trampled somewhat, leaving it easy to climb over. It was loose enough to allow a person to step over, but tight enough to still keep cattle in.

It was a common practice, in days gone by, for farmers and landowners to allow local families to gather twigs and small broken branches along hedgerows. These twigs were not used to *feed* a fire or burn in a fireplace or range, but to get the fire up and burning initially. To kindle it. Hence the word, 'kindling'. To get the fire going, a bit of rolled-up paper was placed in the grate and some dry kindling was added. Then when that was set alight, some coal or turf was added and soon the fire was fully alight. This was in the days when no-one had central heating, either oil-fired or gas-fired.

If a fire is to be lit nowadays, nobody gathers kindling; they just buy a packet of firelighters.

It was just before Christmas, about seven o'clock on a Saturday night. The temperature was below freezing and there were flurries of snow every so often. Not the kind of scene you would see on the front of a Christmas card on the mantelpiece, where the robin sits on a snow-covered post and Santa Claus with his beaming smile and red nose and flowing whiskers, together with his similarly red-nosed reindeer, are in full flight up in the corner of the card. And of course, there's a blazing fire warming the whole scene and the card says *'Happy Christmas'*.

No, this was no Christmas-card scene. This was a cold night, with a biting wind. A night when no self-respecting robin would stick his beak out from wherever he was sheltering.

Mickey, having put on his coat, left through Maggie's back door and stepped over the loose fence behind the house and began walking along the hedge, tramping through frozen grass and rushes in his quest for kindling. As his eyes got used to the darkness, he began gathering twigs and broken branches, squeezing them tightly under his arm as he went along. He intended going just as far as he needed to until he had a good armful, which he would tie with a cord, throw over his shoulder like a swag and return home. He had gone about one hundred and fifty yards, gathering as he went along. Eventually, he reckoned he had enough. Now this night's harvest was not for that night's fire. These twigs were for two or three days ahead. They had to dry out, so people always kept a two-or-three-day supply in stock. By the time they were needed, they were usually well dried out.

Mickey put the twigs and sticks on the ground, pulled a length of old twine from his pocket and proceeded to roll the branches and twigs under his knee, getting them into a tight, manageable bundle, and tied it with the twine. As he was about to swing it over his shoulder, out of the corner of his eye he spotted something unusual. He turned and looked over the wire fence into the thick of the hedge, where he thought he saw, at first, a log. But with a lady's shoe on the end of it. He dropped the twine and took a closer look and lo and behold, what he saw scared the living daylights out of him. He could see that it was no log.

It was a woman's leg, complete with stocking and high-heeled shoe, sticking out of the hedge between the two fences, pointing straight up. He couldn't see any more of a body. Just the leg. So he presumed, correctly as it happened, that the rest of her body was hidden in the hedge by all kinds of growth.

Mickey left the kindling and ran as fast as he could along the frozen ground, until he reached Maggie's, where, almost out of breath, he related what he had just seen.

Perhaps it was on old tailor's dummy, someone suggested.

After some discussion, one of Maggie's sons volunteered to go back with Mickey to make sure he hadn't been seeing things.

So Mickey and the boy headed back down the field, staying close to the hedge, this time with a bicycle lamp with them. When they reached the place where the bundle of twigs still lay, they could see the leg and shoe, just as Mickey had described it. They examined the leg as closely as they could, peering through the wire fence, without disturbing anything. If it was a person, it was clear that she was dead, so there was no point in attempting to save her. But they were convinced – it was no dummy.

They knew enough to touch nothing until the authorities came, so they initially hurried back home and told their story. Yes, it was a body of a woman they were sure, and she was definitely dead. On Maggie's orders, Mickey then left and headed straight for our house. Mickey was sent to our house for two reasons: one, it was 'our' field and two, we were the nearest and only house in the immediate area to have a telephone.

Mickey soon reached our front door and knocked. My father answered the door and Mickey blurted out his story, that there was a dead woman in the hedge, 'over there'. He then left, whereupon my father closed the door and lifted the telephone receiver and soon was speaking to the local Garda station.

At that time, the Garda station (or barracks, as it was usually called) was manned twenty-four hours a day and having got through, via the local manual telephone exchange, he told the officer on duty the broad outline of Mickey's story. The garda said he would get hold of the sergeant and get back to us.

A short time later, the phone rang and the local sergeant was put through. He said that he had spoken with headquarters in Letterkenny and they had said that as it was very late now and if the woman was indeed dead, they would leave things until the morning, when a better assessment of the situation could be established. He told my father to make sure no-one went near the scene before the authorities arrived in the morning. How my father was supposed to do that, I often wonder. And why no officer was sent to guard the scene is puzzling. Yes, it was a bitterly cold night, but Carrigans wasn't Siberia and the gardaí had coats and hats. It was surely their duty to immediately investigate?

But the sergeant ended by saying that they would come to our house at a particular time in the morning and, "We'll take it from there."

By Sunday morning, it was the talk of the village, even before the gardaí arrived. No doubt, the operator in the local manual telephone exchange had their third ear in gear the previous night. And of course, Maggie Brown and her family knew all about it too.

So the story had spread like wildfire by the time the authorities arrived. At about nine o'clock in the morning, a Garda car pulled into our front drive and two officers alighted from the vehicle. My father's memory was that they introduced themselves as an inspector and possibly a sergeant, both from Letterkenny. My father couldn't remember the names. The local sergeant, who my father of course personally knew, opened the back door of the car and alighted. He had obviously been picked up in Carrigans by the Letterkenny men on the way through.

My father ushered all three into our house through the front door.

The first important duty was left to my mother who produced the 'good' tea-set and boiled the kettle. Tea was made, and a plateful of home-made scones followed by an assortment of biscuits was left on the table, together with butter, jam, milk, sugar, etc. All served from her best china in the cupboard. However, this tea-drinking exercise was not just politeness, but a chance by the three garda officers to gather as much of the background story as possible, before heading off to where the body lay. They wanted to know as much as they could before talking with Mickey and then visiting the scene of the body.

Having been amply fed and watered, the three gardaí opened the boot of their car and produced three set of wellingtons, into which they changed, leaving their shoes in the car. At the same time, my father retrieved his wellingtons from the back scullery and pulled them on. They headed off walking the short distance to Maggie Brown's house, where Mickey was waiting. Then, all five, the three gardaí, my father and Mickey, stepped over the loose wire fence and took the same path, more or less, that Mickey had trod the previous night. As they walked, my father recalled, the three gardaí hardly spoke, but closely examined the ground as they walked.

When they reached the place where the leg was protruding, they all had a quick look, before my father and Mickey retreated somewhat, out of earshot of the three officers. No-one made any attempt to approach or touch the leg, which was still in a similar position as Mickey had found it the previous night. One of the officers commented that footprints could be seen approaching the fence from the other side, i.e. from the Northern side. There were footprints on the Southern side also, but it was accepted that these were Mickey and the boy's from the previous night.

After a short conversation among themselves, the inspector asked Mickey if the leg was in the exact same position as it had been the previous night, to which Mickey replied that it was.

Mickey was asked a few more cursory questions – what time he thought it was when he discovered her, the reason for his being there, etc., etc. – and his answers were scribbled down by one of the gardaí in his small notepad.

Mickey was told that he may be contacted in due course just to make a formal statement, and advised not to go back near the body. Mickey then left, retracing his steps of the previous night. The two officers from Letterkenny and my father left the field by a different gate, closer to our house, rather than back through Maggie Brown's. The local sergeant was told to remain at the scene, pending developments. The inspector told my father that, because it was his field, they would be in contact with him also in due course, just to officially confirm that it was his property. So after a further round of handshakes and the changing of the footwear, the two officers left in their car.

About three hours later they returned, knocked at our door, and my father was a little surprised to see them back so soon. They were invited into the house again, but an offer of more tea was refused, with thanks. They all stood in the hall, where they removed their hats and after a moment or two, the inspector asked my father to again confirm that the field was his property and that the adjoining field in the North was not belonging to him. He also asked my father if he had any accurate maps of the property, which might show the actual line of the boundary. My father replied that he hadn't, and if there was a map anywhere it would most likely be in the solicitor's office, along with the deeds.

My father told him that the border was somewhere in the middle, between the two fences. But he added that he had no idea where the actual line was. Nor was there any way he could know, he said, adding that in his humble opinion no-one could determine the exact legal boundary line.

With that, the inspector told my father that he had spoken to his superintendent in Letterkenny, who determined that, as footprints which they presumed were the deceased's were seen on the frosty ground on the Northern side of the fence, it seemed obvious that the woman had approached from the Northern side, attempted to climb over the first fence not realising the extent of the gap between the two fences and had fallen into the scrub in the middle, was unable to extricate herself and subsequently died of exposure.

He now was about to enjoy his *pièce de résistance,* as he stood a little straighter and adopted a more formal pose. As no person, he stated, had been reported missing from his jurisdiction, nor had he received any report of a missing person, and that the deceased person, who was the subject of this short investigation had not actually entered the Republic proper, it was not a matter for him or the Garda Síochána, but was a matter for the police in the North.

In the North, the police were formally known as the Royal Ulster Constabulary, or the RUC for short. The inspector had also, he stated, taken the liberty of directing them to our house, as it was the nearest point of access to the scene, through the nearby gate. Of course, he said, this all was subject to my father's permission to park and indeed to access the body through our field. He asked my father if he would give permission for the RUC officers, should they wish to do so, to park in our yard and cross our field. My father replied, "Of course."

As a result of my father having no objection, the inspector asked if he could use our telephone. My father again said, "Of course," whereupon the inspector lifted the receiver, turned the handle and was connected to the exchange immediately. He asked the operator for a Letterkenny number and again, in a surprisingly short time, he was talking to the station telephone operator. He asked for 'the Chief', again a click, and he was straight through. He just said, "That's okay, sir," and hung up.

My father assumed, quite rightly, that at that very moment, a call was being made from Garda HQ in Letterkenny to the Police HQ in Derry.

Now, it must be stressed that there were no Troubles in the North or the South at that time. The RUC could not, of course, cross the border willy-nilly, nor could the Gardaí. However, as long as it was done in a quiet manner – between two neighbouring headquarters, no uniforms, official cars, or the carrying of arms, etc. – then it happened frequently, where co-operation was vital. Especially in cases where there were no political overtones.

Only then did the group, on my father's invitation, take seats in the kitchen once again, as they waited for the police.

About twenty minutes later, an unmarked car with Northern number plates arrived at our house and after a brief word with the senior garda officer at the front of the house, was directed round to the back. Not that there was any danger; it was just to keep nosey-parkers from seeing it. Two officers in plain clothes got out, came into the house through the back door, more introductions and handshakes all round and, of course, the good cups and saucers were brought out again and the kettle boiled. The two gardai, this time, agreed to accept my mother's hospitality and they accompanied the policemen in a cup of tea.

My father told me that the woman in the hedge was never mentioned during this time. All that took place was a general light-hearted conversation, the weather being the main topic and of course Christmas.

It was first-name terms all round between the officers from North and South. My father told me that he was of the opinion it wasn't the first time that the two senior officers had met. They were very friendly with each other, but I suppose they would be anyway. After all, they were at the end of the day all policemen.

Eventually, the garda inspector rose to his feet and donned his cap, followed by his fellow officer. The Northern police followed suit and after a vote of thanks was proposed to my mother for her hospitality and a plethora of "after you, no after you," all went outside. The RUC officers went out the back door again, opened the boot of their vehicle and donned their wellingtons and heavy overcoats. The gardaí and my father put their wellingtons back on and together, my father and the two officers from Letterkenny and the two policemen from Derry all headed, all five of them, to the scene, where the local sergeant was still standing in the cold, at this stage something akin to Lot's wife.

This time, they entered the field through the gate beside our house. During my conversations with my father in later years, he told me that the local sergeant told him subsequently that the inspector from Letterkenny formally asked the RUC officers, out of earshot from my father, if they were armed. They assured him that they were not, nor had they any arms in their vehicle.

After five minutes, they got to the fence and the hedge. Only then did the everyday conversation cease and a serious approach was taken. No-one spoke, and only the RUC officers took any great interest. The leg was still sticking up, just as Mickey had found it the previous evening.

The gardaí stood back. They had obviously seen all they needed to see earlier.

The two policemen then hopped the fence a few yards up from the body, where it was easier to cross, stepped across a

122

now narrower part of the hedge, climbed down the other side and walked back towards the body. They didn't approach the body but took a wide berth, studying the paths of the footprints, which the woman had made, or which someone else might have made. They talked low amongst themselves, and my father and the gardaí stood speaking in normal tones about this and that, mainly in an effort to show that they were not trying to listen to the policemen's conversation.

Eventually, the two policemen came back over the fence and the senior RUC officer announced that, as far as he could determine, the woman had reached the hedge, that part of which was, in his opinion, in the Republic. And also, he declared, given that the man who found the body was from the Republic, and seeing that the Garda Síochána had been notified first and given that the Gardaí had examined the scene earlier, the affair was, in his opinion, the responsibility of the authorities in the Republic of Ireland.

As such, he declared, the Royal Ulster Constabulary had no further input to make.

So it was a stalemate.

No agreement could be reached as to whether the body was in the North or the South, so neither force wanted the responsibility. Or more likely, the bother.

After all, it was Sunday also. And cold.

At no time was the poor woman mentioned or questions asked about her fate.

It was at this stage that my father left the scene. Now whether he was asked to take his leave, while unofficial talks took place, or not, he never said to me. But he told me that looking back he could see the two senior officers deep in conversation and away from the other three junior officers.

I suspect that he was 'invited' to make himself scarce, while discussions took place.

Five minutes after he got home, the RUC officers and gardaí arrived back at our house, changed out of their wellington boots and into their shoes, but didn't come in and declined the offer of more tea. After another round of handshakes and thanks to my mother and father, they all left.

My father's recollection was that a garda on a bicycle from Carrigans arrived soon afterwards and took up sentinel duty beside the body for the rest of the evening, relieving the local sergeant. My father said that the sergeant said that the local garda, who was watching over the body, told him that a van had later approached from the North just before dark and parked at a spot which, although the closest it could get from the Northern side, was still about two hundred yards from where the body lay. Two men carried a rolled-up type stretcher across the field to where the body lay, eventually got the remains from the thicket, placed them on the stretcher and covered them with a sheet. They carried it to the van, reversed out of laneway where they had parked and drove off towards Derry. Who the men were, whence they came or where they went, nobody knew. The garda, it seems, left on his bicycle shortly afterwards. He never spoke to the two men, nor they to him, although all could see each other.

Nothing more about the whole episode was mentioned, publicly anyway.

And that's more or less where the story ends. But years afterwards, perhaps thirty years later or so, when my father was telling me the story, he did tell me that he had been asked to come to the barracks in Carrigans a few days later. He was told by the local sergeant that they were closing the file on the incident, and they just wanted my father to sign a paper to confirm that the field was his and that no damage was done during the investigation. After confirming this and signing a document to that effect, the sergeant literally closed the file on his desk. The conversation then took an unofficial track and confidentially, he told my father that the woman was indeed from Derry. She had got lost, while endeavouring to meet up with a gentleman. She had become disorientated and, it seems, tried to climb the fence not realising there was a second fence, and probably got caught in the barbed wire, falling over and eventually dying from hypothermia.

Whether this supposed meeting was an illicit one or not, was not mentioned.

Not by my father to me, anyhow.

How the sergeant knew this, my father didn't say. But it seems someone from the woman's family informed the police in Derry that a female sibling had been missing since the Saturday night; the police put two and two together and soon it was confirmed that the woman who was declared missing was the same woman whose body Mickey found in the hedge. There was talk of alcohol, my father said. What he meant exactly, I didn't ask, I presume he meant she was intoxicated.

She was, it was said, in her thirties. A mature woman, I thought, when I was very young. But now when I'm, shall I say, in my advanced years, thirty seems so young,

Just a girl, really.

So the matter was obviously dealt with in a quiet manner. The woman's body, it seems, was retrieved by the authorities in the North, taken to the morgue and then returned to the family home. A death notice in the local paper probably stated that the *'sudden death had taken place of Miss or Mrs. So-*

and-So', a quiet funeral was held and that was that, done and dusted.

No need for any gossip. What her name was, the sergeant never volunteered to my father. Maybe the sergeant knew, maybe he didn't.

The location of her body was not far from the unapproved road, which was made impassable to foot or motorised traffic, having been blown up by the Northern Ireland authorities, and the hole filled with razor-sharp wire. This was following the IRA's 1956 border campaign. As the road was unused, it was a favourite place for lovers to meet. Cars would drive out of Derry, park up and, in general, it was a quite private spot to stay for an hour or so.

In years gone past, the incident never caused me a second thought. But in recent years, several things about this sad affair come to my mind.

What was going through the poor woman's head, when she discovered that she was lost and attempting to find her bearings, but ended up freezing to death on a bitterly cold winter's night?

Was she afraid?

Did she cry out?

She was, at that point, about four miles from Derry. How did she get there?

Where was she attempting to get to?

If this happened nowadays, everything would have to be done officially, everyone would know the name of the woman. Every 'i' would have to be dotted, every 't' would have to be crossed, and proper paperwork documented and completed.

And of course, apart from the official papers, it would be on everyone's Facebook page.

But in those days, 'common sense' prevailed, and the matter was cleared up quietly and efficiently.

If it looked like there was no crime, then there was no need to create a crime.

All, I suppose, to prevent any embarrassment to the woman's family.

As I write about this now, more than sixty years after the incident, I am of the opinion that the local police, North and South, knew very well the circumstances of how and why the poor woman was dead in the hedge, that night.

If either force had to *officially* deal with the matter, then initially there would have had to have been an *official* determination as to which jurisdiction the body actually lay in. This could have taken ages and all sorts of legal paperwork, in both jurisdictions, so I believe that both the RUC Head Constable in Derry and his Garda counterpart, the Superintendent in Letterkenny, would have been wise old foxes and would have known the 'right' thing to do – all in the course of *entente cordiale*, no doubt.

Few speak about this tragic event now and I suspect even fewer know about it. There's no-one left in the locality who was alive at the time and all that remains is what I have written here. And the unanswered questions.

Looking back now, I wonder what the chances are of someone dying or being found dead on the actual boundary line between two different jurisdictions. Right on the border.

Did she die in the North or did she die in the South?

Or did she, in fact, die there in the hedge at all?

And, of course, there is the old euphemistic question – did she fall, or was she pushed?

Or was it just a bit of bad luck?

We shall never know.

5

The Washing Machine

A large international smuggling operation runs into trouble.
But from whom?

In the dining room, the clock on the mantel ticked slowly. It always does, doesn't it, when you're waiting for the time to pass? My mother was sitting in her chair, knitting, her ever present pair of aluminium crutches beside her, while my father, on the other side, was busy switching channels as usual. He had an early version of a remote control. But it wasn't that remote. It was connected to the television by a wire. How many times my mother almost tripped on that bloody wire!

Although we called it the dining room, we seldom if ever dined in it. We lived in it.

Our house was relatively new, and we had a kitchen for cooking in, naturally, a dining room for dining in, and a drawing room for withdrawing to after you've eaten. Or for entertaining 'important' people, whoever they were! But we were different. We cooked and ate in the kitchen, lived in the dining room, and never withdrew to the drawing room.

The hands of the clock reached a quarter to eleven.

"Go on now, you better be on your way," said my mother. "And don't be long," she added as I got up from my chair.

My father followed suit and we left, saying we'd be back in less than half an hour.

It was pitch dark outside, an ideal night for the job. I climbed into the old van while my father got into his car. We didn't switch on the lights of either vehicle until we reached the road, well away from the house. This was an operation not to be undertaken lightly at this hour, or indeed at any hour. You had to be very careful, as failure could land you in jail. Smuggling was illegal and the penalties, if caught, were severe.

But this was no gun-running job, nor had we a lorryload of explosives to transport. We weren't smuggling a hundred crates of illegal whiskey, or a load of drugs from Colombia from a guy called Escobar. (The bad guy in the Colombian cartels is always called Escobar, isn't he?)

The IRA was not involved in this clandestine operation. Nor was the UVF.

No, this was a much bigger job, in our minds anyway.

Tonight, we were smuggling a washing machine.

Yes, one solitary washing machine. An automatic washer and spin dryer, to take the drudgery out of washing and drying the clothes that my mother went through every day, even though she was crippled with arthritis and needed her trusty crutches to get around.

But while it was 'only' a washing machine, it was still a risky business. Mobile customs units were everywhere, as were Garda patrols on the Southern side and British army and RUC patrols on the Northern side. So we had to be very careful. A smuggling trip had to look like an ordinary trip, but not too ordinary. And all precautions had to be in place, but not too many, in case suspicion was aroused. To succeed was really down to a question of timing, bravado and a bit of good luck.

It was February 1972, and the customs patrols were out in force, every night, patrolling some part of the border. Of course, we didn't tell my mother what we were really smuggling. We told her it was an engine for the DUKW (pronounced 'duck') – the World War II landing craft that my father had successfully converted into a fishing boat for use at Magilligan, because it could go on either land or water. The reason we didn't tell her the truth was simply because the washing machine was to be a surprise. My sister lived in Derry and my mother was going to visit her the next day, so we had arranged to have it fitted and plumbed in, ready to surprise her when she came home.

So, in the dark of night, with my father in front and me behind, we headed for the border.

When Ireland was partitioned in 1921, customs and excise posts sprang up all over the length of the border between the two partitioned portions, at the time simply called the Six Counties and the Twenty-six Counties, now officially called Northern Ireland and the Republic of Ireland.

Apart from the political differences, one of the almost immediate effects of partition was the difference in prices of almost everything one could buy. Smuggling was something which was unheard of before, as Ireland was one jurisdiction, albeit under British rule. And also, being an island, the chances of smuggling from Britain or Europe were zilch a hundred years ago.

Along the new border, over the years, there grew up a sort of semi-professional smuggler, who made a living – and for some, a good living – from smuggling. Every stretch of the border had its well-known smuggler, or band of smugglers. The customs officials, especially the Southern ones, were on a continual hunt to catch these guys. Some smuggling was from South to North, but mostly from North, where prices were cheaper, to South. The bigger operators were in the cattle and sheep smuggling trade and often involved large consignments of livestock.

You have to remember that there were no factories producing fridges, washing machines, vacuum cleaners, televisions or any such household items, in Ireland. Almost all household goods such as these were manufactured in Britain and, if you wanted to import these goods, there was a sizeable duty to pay at the border.

And China?

This was in the day when the only things that you saw with 'Made in China' were wooden pencil cases and school rulers. Nowadays, China manufactures...well, just about everything I suppose.

Around the whole border between Northern Ireland and the Republic, there are more than three hundred crossings. Before we all joined what was then the EEC, now called the EU, approximately five out of every six of these crossings between the South and the North were determined to be 'unofficial' and closed completely, by concrete barriers, barbed wire, bridges and roads blown up, or a combination of some or all of these. This saved on having to erect a customs post at every crossing and employ staff for every one of them. Make one crossing official and block the other five in the local area was the general thinking of the authorities. The closure of many minor roads across the border was also welcomed by the Northern authorities, for obvious reasons. But smugglers had ways and means of circumventing the blocked roads, by going through fields for example, or simply crossing the official crossing point at the dead of night and hoping that the customs patrols were somewhere else. Perhaps chasing after a false scent, which was often laid for them.

I personally knew of an operation where the customs got a tip-off that a load of televisions were to be smuggled across the border on a particular night. So, the customs got their men in place, all prepared and ready, and sure enough, at the time given by the tip-off, the lorry appeared. As they went to stop the lorry, the driver drove on and took the customs on a wild goose chase through every small road in the district. Eventually the customs got him blocked and he was nabbed. They opened the doors of the lorry and, sure enough, there stacked to the roof was a pile of cardboard boxes – and on closer inspection of a couple, they were found to indeed contain TVs. The driver was arrested, taken back to customs HQ and the lorry impounded and driven back to the compound by a customs officer. When the lorry arrived back, several customs officers began to empty it of its load, while the driver was being interviewed. He claimed innocence, stating that the boxes only contained old broken televisions, all for dumping. To their horror, the customs, when they opened the boxes, found it was indeed a load of televisions, but all old scrap ones. The penny dropped with them then. The load of new televisions had gone in another direction, the customs having been sent on a wild goose chase.

"So why did you not stop, if you had nothing to be worried about?" asked the officer in charge.

"I thought ye were the IRA!" retorted the driver.

They had to let him go.

Most of the smuggling which does take place nowadays, is carried out by the 'big operators', the mega-smugglers, many of them with paramilitary connections. The kind of guys you don't want to get mixed up with. The boys who smuggle drugs, cigarettes, laundered fuel, livestock, etc., even people smuggling, and all in lorryload quantities.

Even Escobar wouldn't want to get involved with those boys. No way, Jose.

But in the old days, most smuggling was carried out in a Tom and Jerry scenario. At least the small-time stuff that we knew went on. There are many stories about the antics of the part-time smugglers and their attempts to outwit the customs officers. While a few of these 'Dukes of Hazzard' style stories were true, most were apocryphal.

Then you had smuggling where tragedy ensued. For example, in 1944, on the River Foyle, near the village of Carrigans, two men from the village were smuggling various household goods across the river, but the weight was too much for the small rowing boat and it capsized, throwing the two men into the water.

Their bodies weren't found for over a week.

However, everyone did a bit of smuggling, in one shape or fashion, over the years. It might only have been a pound of butter, or a pair of trousers. I can remember one customs officer who was famous for checking the inside label of a jacket or overcoat, to see if it was Irish-made! If not, then duty had to be paid or possibly the garment seized, as well as a possible fine. But many people, like my own mother, were always trying to keep one step ahead. If a coat or jacket was bought in Derry, my mother would have removed the inside label and replaced it with an Irish one, saved from the remnants of an old, discarded coat. Tyres were also smuggled on a grand scale, simply because they were much cheaper north of the border. But if you did go, say, to Derry, to get a couple of tyres on your car, you had to make sure to drive through mud before you arrived at the customs, to take the new look off them.

Did this really fool the officer on duty when he just waved you through? Or did he just wave you on because he couldn't be bothered coming out to check? Who knows?

The mission this night, as I have said, was to smuggle a washing machine from the North to our home in the South. The machine was ready to be collected at a house, a mile or so on the Northern side of the border. The house was owned by Paddy Doherty, known to one and all as Paddy Blue Jesus– yes, the same Paddy from another earlier story.

A day or so prior to this, my father and I had gone to Derry and spent half a day looking at various models of washing machines. The ones you could get in the South were twice the price and usually made in somewhere like Bulgaria, while the ones in Derry, well, they were the best in the world, or so they claimed. Sure wasn't anything that had a label or a badge saying 'Made in England' good? And to be fair, back then, the product which said 'Made in England' *was* well manufactured.

Anyway, we visited a large store that seemed to sell nothing but household items. A well-dressed man in shirt and tie, who looked like he was the owner, approached us and asked if he could be of any help. My father said, yes, we were interested in buying a washing machine. The man immediately escorted us to the washing machine department. Having introduced himself as Mr. Thompson and also having elicited my father's name, he began to explain the functions of the different models. After giving his opinion as to which one he thought would be best suited to my mother's needs, Mr. Thompson took a piece of paper and withdrew a pen from his breast pocket, scribbled a few figures and then told my father that he was going to give us a 'very special price'.

My father feigned a look of gratitude, but Mr. Thompson wasn't fooling anyone. My father was out before.

But eventually, after a little discount and splitting the difference, a price was agreed and a handshake ensued.

"Now, Mr. McGurk," said Mr. Thompson, as he clicked his pen into gear again and got ready to write, "where would you like us to deliver it to?"

My father says, "Well, we live across the border, so can you deliver it to a house out on the Letterkenny Road, about two miles from here, belonging to a man called Paddy Doherty. You'll see a lane –"

He never got any further.

"Ah, sure I know Paddy well," says Mr. Thompson. "We've delivered to Paddy's a few times before."

It wasn't the first washing machine or fridge or freezer left at Paddy's house, in preparation for a further journey across the border in the dead of night.

After a cash payment and a receipt handed over, there followed another round of handshakes, and off we went, happy with the purchase. Presumably Mr. Thompson equally satisfied. On the way, we stopped at Paddy's house, but he was not at home, so we asked his wife if it would be okay to have a washing machine delivered there that day or the next.

"Aye, surely, no bother," said Mrs. Doherty.

We said we would be back for it on the following Saturday night. So the washing machine was duly delivered to Paddy's house by the shop delivery van the following day, as agreed. It was left in the shed behind his house, awaiting our return a couple of nights later.

Now, at that time, as well as the 'good' family car, we had an old van. It's make was a Hillman Husky. It was a product of the 1950s and it certainly drove like it. The body was rotten, but the engine was good. It wasn't a high van, like a Transit or anything like that, but a sort of half van, half estate car. One of those where the front half is more or less a car and the back an extension into a van, but no higher, and two barn-type doors at the back with windows that were blacked out by the previous owner for whatever reason. But I remember that it was a bloody awkward yoke to lift stuff into and out off, especially heavily laden fish boxes.

The reason my father bought it was to transport salmon from our fishery at Magilligan to the fish markets or salmon dealers, wherever they were on the day. These merchants could be anywhere from Coleraine to Strabane, depending on who gave the best price on the day. Of course, carrying fish in the back of the good family car was a definite no-no, for obvious reasons: firstly, the smell, and also, with so much saltwater and melted iced water sloshing about, that would have destroyed any car in no time.

Hence, the old jalopy. We never bothered to wash it out, so it stank of fish, but sure who cared? I remember the wings were completely rusted through, but it was bought for one purpose and that's all it had to do. When it became completely rotten with rust, it was scrapped, and another cheap replacement was bought.

It stayed at Magilligan during the fishing season, but when the season was over, it too was smuggled across, left in our garage and only brought out on special missions like this. The washing machine was worth more than the old Husky.

So, on the following Saturday night, everything was good to go and we headed off to Paddy's house to collect the contraband. I drove the Husky, while my father drove his own car. When I went to start the van, the engine gave a hesitant turn before firing, but when it did fire, she purred like a Rolls Royce. Well, almost!

It was about half a mile to the border and about another mile and a half to Paddy's house, so we were there in no time. With Paddy, my father and myself all pushing and pulling, we managed to get the heavy washing machine, with the aid of a long plank, into the back of the van – just about. We then covered it with old bags until it was practically invisible. I was surprised to find how heavy it was, as I had never physically moved an automatic washing machine dryer before. Paddy said that there's a big lump of concrete in the bottom, to keep it steady when it spins to dry the clothes.

Sort of ballast, he explained.

Made sense, I supposed.

This wasn't the first washing machine which Paddy Blue Jesus had pushed into the back of a van.

So, with the old Husky laden down in the back, off we went. Down Paddy's short lane to the main road – lights off, of course. Paddy gave us a wave out onto the main road. Only then did we switch on the headlights. The most dangerous part was ahead of us.

Now the prearranged plan was that my father was to drive in front and, when crossing the border, he would continue, but

I was to pull in at the Northern side of the border, in a sort of blind area behind some bushes, where the van couldn't be seen from the Southern side. While I was to wait there, he would drive on in his car as far as the village of Carrigans about a mile and a half away. There he would check that the coast was clear, drive back towards the customs post and, when he was on the last half mile straight before the customs, he would flash his lights twice, turn the car at a junction and return home. When I got the all-clear from the flash of his headlights, I was to proceed as fast as the old yoke would go, to the little crossroads, before turning off to our house. The total distance was only about half a mile from the customs to our house, so it was relatively quick and would only take a minute or so at the most.

As I left Paddy's lane I was afraid, yet excited at the same time. It's funny, but the danger can be a bit exciting. But I had extra protection that night. A small statue of St. Christopher stood sentinel on the dash, stuck solidly to it. I suppose he had to be well stuck down as he was getting it tight enough, carrying a rather large infant Jesus across a river or something, he was bent over by the weight. He looked after us when we were on the road, my mother told me. And I suppose I had no reason to doubt her.

So it was just me and Christy and the infant Jesus against the might of the State!

We proceeded to the border and I pulled in, killed the engine and switched off my headlights, and just sat quietly, watching the tail lights of my father's car fade into the distance, before disappearing altogether as he rounded the distant bend.

"We're on our own now," I whispered to St. Christopher.

He didn't answer me, but just stood there glowing in his soft green luminescence.

In those days, we all – well, all of us who were good Catholics anyway – had a St. Christopher in our car. It might have been a picture of him hanging from the mirror, or a small statuette stuck on the dash. How anyone knew what he looked like still puzzles me, given that he died about seventeen hundred years ago! But they told us that he kept us safe in our cars. At least he kept the Catholic drivers safe; the Protestants didn't believe in that sort of idolatry.

I often wondered if Protestants had more car crashes than Catholics, because they didn't believe in St. Christopher. If St. Christopher and the baby Jesus really looked after us, then we had to be safer. Sure it made sense. But then maybe the Protestants made up for it by driving a bit more carefully.

These thoughts ran through my mind as I sat there, waiting in complete silence and darkness. Whatever the statue of Christy and the baby was made of, it glowed in the dark. So there he stood, for all to see. Somebody once said that all these glowing things had radioactive stuff in them, which made them glow in the dark.

I began counting the seconds until my father's return.

I looked up into the sky, but there wasn't a star to be seen. They were all covered by an overcast sky, which was just what we wanted for our operation. The darker it was for a job like this, the better. I could see, however, fleeting glances of the dim moon as the clouds passed it.

Then for some reason, as I looked up at the moon, *Apollo 13* and the guys in the stricken capsule came to my mind. For a minute I felt almost like them, just over a year or so ago, going round the dark side of the moon and losing radio contact with Earth. Like them, I was on my own, with nothing but silence. I wondered if those astronauts were as frightened as me? Probably not. They were used to these sorts of things. One car did approach, before speeding on through, while I kept my head down – literally. I sat in complete silence again for a few more minutes.

Eventually, through a gap in the bushes, I saw a pair of headlights approach from the Southern direction, flash twice and do a U-turn at the junction, before heading back to our home. That was my father and it looked like everything was okay. There were no customs patrols out, in this area anyway, it seemed.

"Right, let's go," I said to St. Christopher, as I turned the key on in the dash (these yokes had no steering locks) and pulled the starter knob. But to my horror – nothing, except a half turn of the engine and then two clicks from the solenoid. The battery was dead…

"Holy fuck," I said to myself.

I held my breath, counted to three, pleaded with the engine– and St. Christopher – then tried again…Nothing.

"Come on, Christopher, not now. Jesus, not at this time," I pleaded.

He either didn't hear me or he didn't want to hear me, but whichever the reason, he was no help when it came to a flat battery. I suppose to be fair, that would have been out of his remit anyhow. Now I had a real problem. There I was, all alone, except for those useless pair glowing on the dash!

"Some fucking good you are now, when I need you," I said, as I gathered my thoughts.

At least the Apollo guys had some power in their service module to get them home. But I had nothing, not a spark – and their mission wasn't half as dangerous as mine. They weren't smuggling a washing machine over the border.

I tried once more, but nothing. I sat there in total silence, wondering what to do next.

I looked at St. Christopher one last time, hoping for inspiration, but he just ignored me. He just stood there, holding his big bent stick.

After a few seconds, I decided to check the terminal connections on the battery, just in case one was loose, but deep down I knew that that was not the problem. The battery had given trouble like this before. I pulled the catch, the bonnet snapped up an inch and stepping out, I walked to the front of the van and proceeded to lift the bonnet and click in the bar to keep it up. I had no sooner pushed it into its slot, when a voice, not more than six feet from me in the hedge, spoke out of the darkness, in a quiet but measured tone.

"Stand fucking still, mate. Put your hands up on the bonnet and if you make one wrong move, you're fucking dead. DO IT – NOW!"

I froze and did exactly as I was instructed. I knew a British army accent when I heard one and I was wise enough to know that if a British soldier ordered you to stand still, you stood still. The Troubles were at their height, and the country was littered with corpses of persons who were ordered to stand still and didn't. You didn't argue with a British soldier, and you certainly didn't argue with one who more than likely had a loaded SLR automatic rifle pointed at you from just six feet.

And Bloody Sunday was only a couple of weeks prior to that night. The country was on edge. So I did what I was ordered to do, no matter what. I stiffened…with my hands up.

At that time, British soldiers, especially in the border region, were well known to shoot first and ask questions later. Whether they were trigger happy or in fear of an ambush, who knows. Probably a mixture of both. It really doesn't matter who's right or wrong if you are lying dead on the roadside.

So I stood statue still and said nothing. No one spoke to me and there was deathly silence. I reckoned he must be behind the old gate pillar in front of the van.

After a few moments I spoke quietly. "It's ok, I'm not a terrorist."

"Don't speak," the Voice said quietly.

So I didn't speak.

All sorts of fears and thoughts went through my head. My biggest fear was of my father driving back towards the customs, flashing his lights. That would certainly spook them. Or another car happening on the scene and slowing down to see what was going on.

Still no-one spoke. Then after about thirty seconds, which seemed like an eternity, the Voice in the hedge, very close to me, said quietly, "So what's in the wagon, Paddy?"

I said, "Please don't shoot, sir. It's only a washing machine for my mother. I'm smuggling it."

I was absolutely trembling with fear.

"You on your own, or is anyone with you?" he asked.

"Yes, sir. I mean no, sir. My dad has gone on to check that there are no customs patrols out. Please don't shoot," I added pleadingly.

"Say again," he said.

"Please don't sh–" I repeated, but he cut me off.

"What did you say about your dad?"

"I said my dad's gone on ahead to check if the road is clear of customs men," I repeated.

Then I could hear the crackle of a hand-held radio.

"Mike Papa, Mike Papa, what's with the van? Over."

The Voice behind me pressed his radio button.

"Alpha Niner Zero, Alpha Niner Zero, a young Paddy. He says he's smuggling a washing machine for his mother."

After a few moments silence, the radio crackled again, *"Say again, did you say a washing machine?"*

"Roger," said the Voice

"Is he on his own?" crackled over the radio.

"Roger," the Voice answered.

Another few moments of silence. The silence was the most frightening time.

"Roger. Check it out."

"Roger."

The radio went silent. From behind the gate pillar, the Voice now appeared. He was dressed in full combat gear, complete with beret and blackened face. Suddenly a red torch was shone in my face and his rifle was pointed at me.

"So, what's your name, Paddy?"

"McGurk," I says, "Frank McGurk."

"Where do you live?"

"Just over there, about half a mile away." I pointed with the nod of my head backwards.

Again, silence. The silence was the most frightening part of the time. I was still standing in front of the van, my hands up on the bonnet. He was now behind me.

"Ok, Paddy." (While I had told him my name was Frank, he still called me 'Paddy'.) "Keep facing the van, leave the bonnet up and walk very slowly round this side of the van –

and keep your hands on the roof of the vehicle. Go to the rear doors and stop when I tell you."

So I sort of crabbed sideways round the van, very slowly, and did everything I was ordered and eventually I was standing exactly like I had been, only this time at the back of the van.

"Stop!" came the order, and then suddenly what felt like the barrel of a gun poked my back and hands were frisking me up and down, in and out, but by a different soldier. The Voice stood pointing his gun at my waist.

"Open both doors, one at a time. Slowly," he ordered.

So I slowly opened the two doors back and, as I did so, a torchlight from behind me lit up the inside of the van.

"Ok, so what's that, Paddy?" said the Voice.

"That's the washing machine," I said. "I'm telling you the truth, sir. It's just a washing machine. I'm smuggling it across the border. A washing machine is cheaper in the North, so I'm smuggling it across to our house."

"Where's your house?"

"Just over there, where I told you," I replied, again nodding with my head, this time forwards, in the general direction. "Please come and check it yourself, sir. It's only a washing machine. We threw the rags over it just to make it less noticeable."

Silence again.

"Let me be absolutely clear. If you make one wrong move, I'll shoot you. Do you understand?" said the Voice.

"Yes, sir, absolutely clear," I said. "But I'm telling you the truth, I have nothing in the van that I shouldn't have. Please don't shoot."

"If you do as you're told and you're not carrying anything illegal, you've nothing to fear," he says matter-of-factly. "Now, take those rags off it and turn it around."

"I can't by myself," I said. "It's too heavy, there's concrete in the bottom."

"Concrete? In a washing machine?" said the Voice, with a touch of scepticism.

"He's right, sir," said another soldier, from a few feet away. "They do have concrete in them."

"It's to stop it jumping all over the place, when it spins the clothes dry…sort of ballast," I added, echoing Paddy's words.

The other soldier nodded.

That diffused the situation a little. A red torch was switched on again.

The officer behind me beckoned the other soldier to come over, which he did.

"Stand here," the Voice then said to me, pointing to a spot on the ground about three feet from the van. "And keep your hands up."

As I moved aside, I saw the other two soldiers for the first time. They were also in full combat gear, complete with battle gear, totally blackened faces and wearing dark berets.

"Turn the machine round," said the Voice to one of the other squaddies.

So one of them climbed into the back of the van on his knees and pulled the old bags off the washing machine. A spanking brand-new machine presented itself in the torchlight. The soldier shone his torch through the glass door and all around the drum.

"Don't open it," said the Voice. "We'll let Paddy do that."

The soldier inside then backed out of the van.

"Seems okay, sir," he said as he straightened himself up.

The Voice then ordered me to go into the back of the van and open the door of the washing machine.

I immediately obeyed, pressed the button. The door sprung open.

Another moment passed, then he told me to get out again, which I did. He ordered the other soldier to go back in again and check it out, inside and out. The other soldier did so, running his hand round the inside of the washing machine and knocking the sides of it with his knuckles.

Eventually he spoke to his officer, "It's okay, sir. It's just a washing machine."

My arms were tired, so I went to lower them a little, when the voice snapped at me, "Keep your hands up!"

It was the first time he had raised his voice to me in anger. I thought, perhaps he was annoyed that he didn't find anything else.

"Check out the rest of the van," said the Voice to the soldier in the van.

"Yes, sir."

Meanwhile a couple more soldiers had appeared from nowhere, all blackened faces and stopping a couple of cars, going in both directions. I reckoned that there was about six of them in this patrol. One of them approached the Voice and whispered something in his ear.

"Yes, sir, absolutely," said the Voice.

I reckoned this new soldier was the commanding officer of the whole group.

"Sir, may I speak?" I said to the Voice.

After a moment, he looked at me and said, "Yes, you can speak now."

"Sir, my dad will be worried and probably will come back to see why I'm still here. Please don't shoot. I don't get mixed up in that sort of thing."

"What sort of thing?" he queried.

"Guns and that sort of stuff," I replied.

"You don't get mixed up in that kind of thing, you say. So what do you work at?"

"I work in a bank," I said. "I'm a bank official."

The torch continued to shine right into my face. Then suddenly he shone it downwards.

"Show me your hands," he said, "both sides."

He could see I was no tractor mechanic. The torch went off.

Suddenly the soldier inside the van called out, "Fucking hell!" before emerging backwards from the van.

Everyone, including myself, froze.

"He's been carrying more than washing machines, sir," he said. He then bent over and retched. About three red torches shone in my face. The situation suddenly turned scary.

"So, what else have you been carrying then? Drugs?" asked the Voice.

"No sir, nothing sir, nothing," I pleaded.

"What have you found?" asked the Voice, keeping his torch trained on me, but directing his question to the other soldier.

"Nothing there now, sir. But he's been carrying rotten fish of some kind," the other soldier replied, as he retched again. "It's fucking stinking in there."

One of the other soldiers let out a slight laugh. The situation calmed again. The Voice shone the torch back into and around the van and then back on me. As he did, he called, "Right, let's go, men."

Turning to me, he said, "Sorry for the hold up, sir, safe home – with your washing machine."

The torch went off and he and the other soldiers went to walk away into the darkness.

"Sir," I called after him.

They all stopped and look around and the Voice said, "What is it?"

"I need a push," I said quietly.

There was no reply for a moment. Then the Voice laughed, the first time he did so.

"He needs a push. Paddy needs a fucking push," another soldier beside him said.

Somewhere behind came another laugh.

"Paddy's out on a smuggling run and he needs a fucking push!"

They all laughed before the commanding officer barked, "Quiet."

I said to no one in particular, "She won't start. Remember, that's why I was still here. My battery's flat."

The torch almost blinded me and there was silence again. The Voice didn't speak for a moment.

"I do need a push – please."

The Voice readjusted his beret, hesitated for a moment, looked at his commanding officer, who nodded his head, then said, "Right, come on, you two," motioning to two other soldiers. He switched off his torch and clipped it to his belt.

After closing the back doors and dropping the bonnet gently, I got into the van. I realised that I was now more frightened than I was all the time they held me. Supposing the van backfired? I remembered a workman's van backfired in Belfast a few months before and the army shot him dead.

Harry somebody or other.

Or supposing they let me go a hundred yards and then opened up? I glanced at St. Christopher, but he just stood there, mute. He had nothing to add.

"We'll try it in reverse," said the Voice.

"Why reverse?" I asked.

The soldier continued. "See that line there, where the two roads meet. We can't cross that. That's the Irish Republic. We're not allowed to cross over there."

As if I didn't know! I could have said that it wasn't the first time the British army crossed the border, but I held my tongue, naturally. Not the time to be smart, I reckoned.

So three of them went to the front of the van and began to push the van backwards. It was absolutely no effort for three fully fit British soldiers.

It's funny what comes into your mind at strange moments. Earlier, when the van wouldn't start and I was sitting in complete silence, I had thought of the men in *Apollo 13*. But just now, as the three blackened faces looked at me through the windscreen, I had a sudden flashback of an old black-and-white war film I had seen, in which British soldiers were pushing a lorry backwards up a sand dune in the desert.

I put the van in gear and held her on the clutch and switched on the ignition. I was absolutely terrified. Then the van began to move a little faster. All I could hear was the sound of boots running. I let the speed pick up a bit and then let in the clutch with a snap. The van started immediately. But somewhere along the line, I must have switched on the headlight switch. So when the engine fired into life, the lights suddenly went on full beam and there I could see, in front, like proverbial rabbits, three soldiers, in full illumination.

"TURN THOSE FUCKING LIGHTS OFF!" they roared in unison.

I turned the lights off post-haste. The window was already down, so I said, "Sorry, I didn't know that the light switch was on. Thanks very much."

The Voice came over to the open window.

"Right, away you go, Frank. Goodnight and safe home," he said to me in the darkness. It was the first time he called me by my proper name.

"Goodnight and thanks again, sir," I replied, as I drove away, slowly.

I didn't know if it was the right thing to do or not, but when I pulled away, I gave the horn two short beeps. The next three hundred yards were the most frightening three hundred yards I have ever travelled. I kept talking to St. Christopher. "We're nearly there. We're nearly there, Christy, just a wee bit more."

He didn't answer, but I knew he was on my side, as we rounded the bend and out of the soldiers' view.

Then, with great relief, I was at the crossroads, and in a few moments I was in the back yard of our house.

As the saying goes, I wasn't worth tuppence. The whole thing only hit me then. But after a moment I was okay and home safely again. Just like the Apollo guys.

As I drove into the yard, my father was just about to get into his car.

"I was just going to look for you. What happened to you?" he asked. "You took long enough."

"Got stopped by the army," I said. "They didn't believe I only had a washing machine. They held me and searched me and the van up and down. But in the end they let me go. They even pushed me," I added.

"Pushed you? You mean they pushed you around?"

"No, they gave the van a push – to get her started. That's why I didn't get away, when you flashed the lights. I went to start the van but the battery was flat. I had to ask the soldiers to give me a push."

He didn't comment, so I added, "Well, I didn't have much choice. Would you rather they weren't there and maybe the customs arrive instead?"

"I suppose not," was his only comment. "We thought the customs had caught you."

I followed him into the house, closed the back door behind me and walked through the kitchen and into the dining room.

"Did everything go okay? Did you get the engine out?" my mother asked.

So I told her the whole story – the flat battery, the soldiers, the searching and the push to get started, of course without mentioning the washing machine. It was an engine for the DUKW, as far as she was aware.

"Did they rough you up or give you a hard time?" she asked.

"No," I said, "to be fair, they didn't. They were okay, they never laid a hand on me, except for a frisking and searching of my pockets. I could hardly see them anyway. They had their faces all blacked out and all I could see, when I saw them in my headlights, was that they wore bright red berets."

When they heard 'red berets', my father and mother looked at me then at each other.

Their faces had turned almost pure white.

Neither spoke.

6
Wake Night

An old man has died.
A young man goes to the wake to pay his respects.

Part One – Chief Cashier

If I remember right, it was late in the year, maybe a bit before Christmas, when I heard the news that Ritchie Porter had died. This would have been about the mid nineteen eighties.

I was sad when I heard it. I hadn't seen Ritchie or his wife in a few years and I had always intended to visit them at their home in Lifford. But the world is full of good intentions, and we tell ourselves that we will do these things we promised ourselves to do, when we get time. We haven't time just now, we're too busy with this, that or the other. So when I heard of his sudden death, I was determined to go to his wake. It was the least I could do.

Ritchie Porter and his wife lived in Lifford. They were a very good and kind couple, maybe too kind. I had only known Ritchie and Mrs. Porter for a couple of short years, from about 1972 to 1974 approximately. I never knew Ritchie before that short period, and I never saw him again after that.

So how did our paths cross for those fleeting couple of years?

To explain, I need to go back a couple of years. To 1970, in fact.

That year, I had applied for and was successful in getting a job in the Munster and Leinster Bank in Omagh, in County Tyrone. The Munster and Leinster Bank was to soon become part of Allied Irish Banks, or AIB. It was my first official job.

I didn't enjoy my time in Omagh, but it wasn't the job I disliked, it was the town itself. And especially my digs.

Having a very strange woman as a landlady didn't help either. In fact, as time went on, I came to believe that she was a complete fruitcake.

She wasn't my first landlady, however. That honour fell to a lady who lived close to the police station. She was a nice woman and a good cook, and I had a cosy room. So, what was the problem, you're asking? The problem was that her husband was an ardent follower and member of the Free Presbyterian Church, Ian Paisley's church, and this man had LP records of Paisley's preachings and he played the records day in day out, at almost full volume.

I didn't stay long there. I couldn't care less about The Reverend Paisley's take on the Gospels or the Epistles – it was the decibels that I couldn't stick.

Somebody told me that a woman on the Derry Road had a nice house and that she took in lodgers. So, one day I went to her house, knocked on her door and this old woman of about fifty years of age, or maybe a tad more, opened the door a fraction. She had a cigarette with the ash still hanging on in her mouth. That should have told me enough. But when I said I was looking for lodgings, she opened the door wider and invited me in. She told me what she normally gets for lodgings, and I said okay. But there was something about her that made me uneasy. But I couldn't put my finger on it. Her name was Sheila something-or-other. I can't remember her surname. The first couple of weeks was fine, but after a while, I felt that she was following me about. She reminded me of Norma Desmond, the old has-been movie star in the film *Sunset Boulevard*. And as time passed, I began to feel like her Joe Gillis, the guy who was being slowly entrapped in her web.

After a couple of months, I got fed up with her. I got fed up with her house, I got fed up with her cooking, I got fed up with her strange behaviour, her incessant smoking – in fact I got fed up with just about everything in that house. So I eventually decided to move elsewhere. But when I plucked up the courage to tell her that I wanted to move on, she didn't want me to go. She begged me to stay, even offering not to charge me any rent. Then, when that didn't work, she even offered to give me money, just to stay. But I knew I couldn't put up with her weird ways much longer and I was determined to get out of there.

To give an example, one day, on his way home from Dublin, my father called to see me at her house. After he left, she called me into the sitting room and asked me if my mother was alive. I thought it was a strange question and I said yes she was alive and asked her why she had asked me that. She said it was because she had fallen in love with my father. After meeting him for two minutes. She asked when he would be visiting me next, so that she could have meal prepared for him. Needless to say, I never asked him to call there again.

That's how unpredictable she was. Years later, my dad laughed when I told him. But I didn't think it was funny at the time, not in the least.

She told me that she was afraid of living on her own since her brother had died. She spent all night walking the floors and chain-smoking her cigarettes. I could hear the creak of every stair, as she went up and down them.

It got to the stage when I didn't sleep well, and I couldn't lock the bedroom door as there was no key. Many nights, I saw the shadows of her feet, under the door. All I could think of was her coming into my room, stabbing me to death and then, when the police and press arrived, she would stand at the top of the stairs and say, "All right, Mr. DeMille, I'm ready for my close up."

I know, I know, I'm getting a little carried away. But I *was* frightened. I ended up placing a chair under the doorknob, in case she tried to come in when I was asleep.

I struggled on a little longer, I just hadn't the willpower to leave. But in the end, I couldn't take any more of her strange habits, so I plucked up the courage and told her I was definitely leaving. She went into hysterics, broke down and cried, so I said I wouldn't go just yet. But one day while she was away shopping or something, I left her a 'Dear John' letter and skedaddled.

But, like Norma Desmond, Sheila didn't give up easily and, the next day, she came into the bank and pleaded with me to go back – in front of everyone. I was so embarrassed.

But I was really beginning to be afraid of her. She even asked the manager, Mr. Moan, to persuade me to go back. To keep her happy, he said he would try.

I wish he had told her to clear off. The staff all laughed at my predicament and made fun of the whole thing, asking me what was it I had, that made her want me back.

Had I, they would ask, a young man of eighteen, something special that made an elderly lady of fifty years old, at least, want me to live with her? I tried not to show it, but deep down I wasn't in the least amused by all this.

Even the chief cashier, Mr. McMahon, got in on the act, telling me with a straight face that she was filthy rich, had no relatives, and I should go back and I'd probably get the lot, when she kicked the bucket – in about forty years! Or better still, he suggested without blinking an eye, "Push her out the upstairs window and you're home and dry! You'll be a millionaire! You'll get her house, her money and probably loads of precious jewellery."

The staff all thought this was very funny.

I didn't.

Not if I was getting a million pounds would I go back and I never did. I could write that she died a broken woman, or in a psychiatric hospital like Norma Desmond, but the fact is I have no idea how she ended up. All I knew was that I was determined not to end up like Joe Gillis. I never set eyes on her afterwards. Although I admit I have mellowed a little in my later years and looking back, I guess the woman was just lonely and perhaps a little afraid on her own and felt safe with me around. So I have some sympathy for her now. Not a lot, but some.

The boarding house I went to next wasn't a whole lot better, however. But that's another story.

Then, in 1971, I had a bit of good luck. A letter arrived on the manager's desk stating that I was being transferred to

Strabane, which was just on the border with Donegal, and my whole life was about to take a real big turn for the better. For a start I was much nearer to where I was from and I could go home almost every night. Sometimes I got a lift, other times my father came to collect me. And, of course, I would come home each evening to my mother's delicious dinner! That was one of the things I missed, when I was in Omagh. There is only one word to describe Sheila's cooking – awful.

So, soon I left Omagh behind me and started work in the Strabane branch one Monday morning in the summer of 1971. Despite the shootings, the bombings and the robberies that were happening day and daily in Strabane, as part of what was called the Troubles, we just got on with the job. In retrospect, I wonder how we managed. But we did.

I had been transferred as a clerk, which meant basically being the 'gofor' in the office – "Go for this, go for that! Get me this, get me that!" But then in 1972, just a few months later, I had another boost. I was promoted to 'Chief Cashier' in the Strabane branch of the Munster and Leinster Bank.

My 'Joe Gillis' days were finally well behind me!

In no time at all, I could see myself being CEO of the whole bank, sitting in a big leather chair in a plush office somewhere in Dublin, with a plethora of secretaries who, as well as typing my letters, would be bringing me chocolate biscuits and glasses of mineral at my every beck and call.

However, fate chose a different path for me and I never did get to sit in the big plush chair in Dublin, with the secretaries attending to my every whim.

Banks in the old days were big into promotions and titled positions, such as Manager, Deputy Manager, Assistant Manager, Chief Inspector, Assistant Inspector, S.B.O, (Senior

Bank Official) Chief Cashier, Junior Teller, Ledger Machinist, Head Porter, etc. Now, being known as the Chief Cashier in the Strabane branch of the Munster and Leinster Bank was a bit of an overkill, the reason being that there was only one cashier in the branch anyway – and that was me. But the job description, plus the sign over my cash booth that said 'CHIEF CASHIER' and the nameplate on the counter that said 'FRANK McGURK', meant I was 'important'. That nameplate meant I *was* somebody. Like a President in the Oval Office, almost, or a judge you would see on 'Perry Mason'!

Well, that's what the bank wanted you to think anyway.

Nowadays, the customer areas in banks are almost all open plan, but in those days it was all booths, with frosted glass and small confessional-like doors, not solely for security, but also for privacy. Every customer could have a one-to-one in the privacy of a booth. My cash booth at the end of the counter was somewhat larger than the others, I suppose to cater for bags of cash and coin, and was even more private. Because that's where cash changed hands and privacy was paramount. If Joe-the-Shopkeeper from up the street was at the cash booth, he wouldn't want Nosey Mary from down the street seeing his business.

Hence the reason for the boxed-in style of booths. The promotion to 'Chief Cashier' gave me a small rise in salary, but in reality it was hardly noticeable as at the end of every month I was broke anyway. In the bank, in the old days, you were paid monthly. Bad idea. It came in one lump, but it disappeared just as quickly. By the time my dues were paid – union fees, insurance premiums paid, etc. – plus money owed, it was gone.

But I always had my father and mother, when things became a little tight. I could always get a small sub from my father, if I needed it, while my mother would give me a couple of pounds every so often, without my asking. She would slip the cash into my pocket. Of course, the 'subs', which I got from my father were never repaid.

But the main big change to my life was that I managed to buy my first car. It was brand new, a yellow Mini, bought in Dublin, and it cost £810. Despite my poverty, I had managed to save £210, mostly from overtime pay earned during the changeover from 'old money' to 'new money' and the manager, Mr. Wall, organised me a loan of £200, while my father donated the other £400 to me. While it was strictly against the bank staff employment regulations to have a loan or borrowings in your own bank, or indeed in any other bank, there were ways around it. No employee of the bank was permitted to be in debt to the bank, unless, of course, he or she had a full authorised mortgage for a house purchase, if say, he or she was getting married. That was permitted. But other than that, you could not have an overdraft or a loan, in your own bank. Or indeed any other.

But there were ways and means.

How staff got round it was this. Almost every employee, from manager down (but not a junior clerk, you had to be the cashier, at least, or an S.B.O), if he needed a few pounds, would get a small loan in another bank down the street, in his surname, but with a different first name and any address that suited. Although, as I say, this was against staff rules, everybody including managers, especially in a medium-sized town where there were half a dozen different banks and all the staff knew one and other, availed of it at one time or another.

Many members of staff had small loans in other banks in a slightly different name. It was all done on the QT, and these loans were for small things like a bit of furniture, holidays, a new suit or maybe a change of car, that didn't involve too much money.

There were reasons for these hush-hush loans.

Firstly, bank staff, especially lower down the pecking order, got very poor pay, so if these small loans helped dress you a bit tidier so much the better. If you worked in the bank in the old days, it was more of a prestige job, rather than a well-paid job. It had the name of an important salaried position. In any town, years ago, the important people were the clergy, the doctor, the solicitor and the bank manager (and staff). People were expected to look up to you. So, if you were thought to be important, then you had to look important.

The second reason we took out these loans was because, as I've already mentioned, we got paid monthly and it was a long time until next payday.

So, Mr. Wall had made a phone call down the street, as I'm sure he had done on many previous occasions, spoke to his opposite number in the other bank and secured the loan, under the name of 'Joseph McGurk' (my middle name). Any address sufficed. I think mine was 'Lifford, Co. Donegal'.

As I have said, it was all very hush-hush, but I soon discovered that almost all the staff of the other five or six banks in Strabane had these small unofficial loans. It was a spider's web of small loans spread across town. It was based on trust – a nod and a wink – and there was no security involved. But no-one ever defaulted. You got the loan and you paid it back.

Strangely enough, only later did I discover from talking to staff members from the 'old days' that almost a hundred percent of these loans were taken out by male staff.

I suppose the thinking was that no female member of staff would stoop to ask for a loan, but then again, if she had a boyfriend, a loan from the bank was hardly needed!

So, I had my brand-new car and I was a happy young man. I put all the extras on – spotlights, radio, rally seats, stripes, and so on – until I had a really 'flash' car. And flash cars meant only one thing – flash women! Well, that was the thinking, anyway. It didn't always work out that way, though.

My main job as 'Chief Cashier' was to manage the cash desk, which entailed balancing the cash incomings and outgoings, together with lodgements and debits. All that mattered was that the cash ledger and the cash itself balanced at the end of the day.

As with most banks, even today, the branch didn't open its doors to the public each morning until 10 a.m. There was a good reason for this. It was to prepare for the coming day, getting out the ledger books, statement files and so on. I suppose nowadays all each official needs to do is switch on the computer.

Between 9 a.m. and 10 a.m., I had no need to be in the cash booth. But I had another job to do during that period.

That second job was called, 'Doing the Morning Letter'.

How it worked was this: thousands of cheques, maybe millions in those days, were written by millions of customers, drawn from banks all over the world.

These cheques eventually find their way back to their country of origin and end up in that country's Central Clearing bank. On arrival there each day, they are separated into their various banks and then the individual branches of each bank. Nowadays, of course, it's mostly all e-banking and the much-reduced number of cheques are sorted automatically in the blink of an eye.

But back then, it was all done by hand. All Irish-drawn cheques – that is, cheques from all banks in Ireland – eventually found their way to the Central Bank clearing centre in Dublin. In Northern Ireland, of course, it was the clearing centre in Belfast. There they were separated and pigeon-holed into the separate banks and then each bank's bundle was further separated into branches of those individual banks. Those that were destined for our bank in Strabane were, after being totalled and debited to Central Bank Clearing account, posted by registered mail to our bank each evening. That sealed letter arrived each morning, by registered mail and was duly signed for.

This was, as I have said, called the 'Morning Letter'. It was my job to open it and withdraw all the cheques, bunch them into a bit of order like one does with a pack of cards, alphabetise them, and then go through them, one by one. After each one was examined, the amount was debited from that customer's account.

But only if that cheque 'passed muster'. And that was my job, before opening time.

I had to check the signature, check the date, check that the amount in numbers and the writing agreed and finally, and most importantly, check that the customer's account had sufficient funds to cover the cheque. Or in the case of an overdraft, that the cheque didn't exceed his or her borrowing limit.

Still with me?…Good.

Our branch had about a hundred or maybe a hundred and fifty cheques, give or take, each morning. If any of these points for examination did not pass the test, for one or more of the reasons described above, there were various options open to me.

Forged signatures were very rare and normally carried out by a family member, and sorted out without too much hassle— but as I say, very rare.

A wrong date was often a genuine mistake, mostly made in the first days of a new year or, if post-dated, then the payee should not have presented it. That's why it was post-dated in the first place. If it was for a small amount, then generally this was ignored.

The most important check, as I say, was to see if the drawer had the wherewithal to stand over it: that they had enough money in their account to cover the amount of the cheque.

Normally, out of, say, the hundred and fifty cheques which would land on my desk, a hundred and forty-five of them, approximately, wouldn't cause me to blink an eye. You got to know all the sound ones and you got to know the iffy ones. Any that needed further scrutiny would be placed to one side.

So, after about half an hour, if I was left with half a dozen cheques that needed further inquiry, I would give them the fine-comb treatment. This was almost always to check if the cheque was payable or not, depending on the solidity of the drawer's account. I got to know the ones which I would place in the 'defer' drawer. This was a kind of Limbo, where the customer's cheque would neither be paid nor refused on that particular day. The cheque got an unofficial day's grace, to allow time for the customer to lodge enough funds to cover it – normally after I had made a discreet telephone call advising them that their cheque could not be honoured and funds would have to be lodged that day. I always added that I was speaking on behalf of the manager. Like old Harry, the buck stopped with him.

Nine times out of ten, things sorted themselves out and the cheque would eventually be passed for payment.

I got to know the 'definitely nots' and these were just sent back whence they came, having been stamped, 'Refer to drawer'. And any that I couldn't decide on were taken into the manager's desk and set down for his decision. The manager had several options at that stage.

Option one, if they were a 'good' customer, he let it go. He knew the score. It would be okay.

Option two, if they were a habitual problem, it was returned – 'Refer to drawer'.

Option three, the manager or myself made a phone call.

Option four, the cheque was put into Limbo for a night – or, on a very rare occasion, depending on the customer, two nights. This option, while technically against bank protocol, was not uncommon practice.

If the customer's general handling of his account wasn't bad enough to deserve the cheque being bounced, but they just hadn't the funds to cover the cheque on the day, then the cheque was put into the Limbo drawer. The important thing about the Limbo drawer was that the cheque wasn't stamped, or 'branded' as we called it. By not stamping it, it could sit until the next day, giving the customer a chance to get things in order. If they did that, then the cheque was paid the next morning, if not, it was bounced. On a very, very rare occasion, as I have already stated, if the person was in general a very good customer and had genuine reasons for not being able to lodge that day, let's say he or she was out of reach, through illness or suchlike, they got the benefit of a second night in the drawer.

As time passed and I got to know the customers, the Good, the Bad and the Chancer, I gradually knew the score and seldom had to consult with the Boss. After a month or so, I knew them all and although technically it was still the manager's call, I had the unofficial authority to make the decision, unless in exceptional circumstances – for example, for a large cheque written by one of our larger companies, which I was not in the position to authorise or refuse.

But that was rare and, in general, if a customer played fair with me I played fair with them. If they didn't, then their cheque never even got to see inside the Limbo drawer. It was bounced quicker than a McEnroe serve.

So, I got to know the routine very quickly and this morning job became a speedy operation. After a short time, I could run my eye over each cheque in two seconds. Of course, while the manager did give me full authority, technically, as I have stated, the default position lay with the manager and it allowed me to say, sometimes, on the phone, "Sorry, Sir (or Madam), but the manager has instructed me to…"

That was me passing the buck.

When a cheque was refused and returned, or bounced, the girl in the back office would write an accompanying letter to whoever had lodged it – sometimes it was one of our own customers but more often it was from another bank. These letters were always signed by the manager.

So, while it might have been me who made the decision to write the dreaded letter, it was the manager who signed it.

Of course, banks today have no such thing as a human being making a decision to return a cheque or not to return. There's no leeway today. In fact, you could say that banks are no longer run by humans. They are run by unknown officials, who take their orders from, as Don McLean sang, 'frameless heads on nameless walls'.

Part Two – Opec

In 1973, while I was still working in Strabane, the leading members of OPEC decided to hit back at those countries that had supported Israel after the Yom Kippur War – mainly the US and the UK. Oil rose from $3 a barrel to over $12 a barrel. On top of that, OPEC held back on distribution in an attempt to 'starve' the West by withholding oil. As a result, there were petrol famines in almost all countries in Europe, including Ireland.

Most of Ireland's petrol came from UK companies. Therefore when the UK suffered, Ireland suffered too – and more so. Ireland would only get the drippings from the barrel, literally.

But I didn't care about Europe, the UK, or even Ireland. The only person I cared about was myself. The rest of the country could want, for all I cared. It was vitally important that I had petrol, partly so that I had transport to my work, but it was much more important that I had enough to allow me to continue with my busy social life.

There were no diesel cars on the road at that time. Only lorries and large vans used diesel. So during the OPEC embargo, queues formed at filling stations for petrol. The bigger the cities or towns, the bigger the queues.

In places like Dublin especially, given the number of cars in the capital, the queues were up to a mile long. In Donegal, the situation wasn't good either. Petrol was very scarce, but it was slightly easier to get than it was in the big cities. Even if your tank was three quarters full and there was an opportunity at a petrol pumps to get a gallon, or even half a gallon, you never passed up on the chance.

But there was no scarcity of petrol as far as I was concerned. No queuing for me. I had more petrol than the Sheik of Oman.

How?

Well, let me tell you. This is where Ritchie Porter enters the tale.

Part Three – Quid Pro Quo

I was lucky, but it wasn't all luck. There was a lot of goodwill between myself and the aforementioned Ritchie Porter.

On my way to my work in Strabane, there was a Shell filling station at Rossgier, about a mile before Lifford, a small town on the Southern side of the border that was twinned with Strabane. Ritchie had taken a lease on the filling station and adjoining house. He was a small man and he always wore a trilby-style hat. Ritchie and his wife reared a large family. As I have said, they were a decent and honourable couple.

Before I got my new Mini, I didn't need petrol, so I had no reason to visit his filling station. But when my new car came on the scene, I got almost all my petrol at Ritchie's, mostly in the evening on the way home, as I was usually late in the morning and hadn't the time to stop. I was a bad riser. A quick wash and dress, a bite of breakfast and away, like lightning.

I was supposed to start work at 9 a.m. but I usually left home about 8.40 a.m., which normally gave me just about enough time, unless there was a queue at the army checkpoint.

Ritchie was also a customer of our bank in Strabane, so I changed my usual habit of stopping in the evening to stopping in the morning. To save Ritchie the trouble of going to the bank, I began the habit of taking his lodgement with me into the branch. While Ritchie was counting it, Mrs. Porter would usually give me a cup of tea – and a slice of toast.

But Ritchie had a problem. Ritchie's sums were slowly but surely failing to stack up. The main reason was not that he wasn't selling enough petrol. No, the sales of petrol were okay. Ritchie's problem was that he was a generous man and a trusting man – too generous and too trusting, especially to too many Johnny good-for-nothings, who were giving Ritchie their business on a see-you-later or tick basis. In other words, Ritchie was giving too much petrol on credit to too many so-called customers, who would get a gallon or two one day, promise to pay the next day, but fail to do so. When they eventually came back, Ritchie gave them more, in the hope of getting all that he was already due. But, as my father used to say, it was throwing good money after bad. When the so-called customer had reached his limit, or more accurately Ritchie's limit, he didn't come back at all, but would get his petrol elsewhere. And Ritchie was left high and dry. So Ritchie would lose both the money owed to him, plus the customer's trade. Ritchie was just that type of good neighbour to too many unreliable customers.

So, that led to the inevitable. There came occasions when Ritchie's income was getting seriously close to his outgoings. While the petrol turnover was remaining steady, the income from sales was slipping.

The scales were beginning to tip.

If Ritchie wrote a cheque that rang alarm bells, I always did my best for him. Now, this would have been a rare occurrence. Ninety-nine per cent of the time, Ritchie was okay, nothing to worry about.

But on the rare occasion that it did occur, I would defer it into the Limbo drawer; in other words, leave it for a day. I would call with Ritchie on the way home and fill him in on the situation.

Ritchie was very grateful for this, and by next morning he would have been in touch with a few of his credit customers. By the time I called, a larger than usual paper bag awaited me and in less than half an hour everything was back on an even keel.

In all my time there, I never had to return a cheque of Ritchie's.

He often told me about the credit he was owed from others, which he knew was more or less a write-off. So I told him that the first thing he needed to do was cut out those clients altogether and stick with the good customers.

"I know it's not easy, Ritchie," I told him. "But you will just have to control your credit sales to the bare minimum."

Ritchie took my advice and within a couple of months his business was doing okay again.

I had helped in a small way to throw Ritchie a financial lifeline on a couple of occasions, and he didn't forget that. So when the OPEC petrol crisis hit, Ritchie came up trumps and paid me back – in spades. The oil sheikhs' embargo came like a bombshell and getting petrol was like finding hen's teeth, all over the country.

Petrol was, as I have said, severely rationed and although, on paper, Ritchie's sales probably dropped in terms of gallons sold, as he simply couldn't get the petrol, his income didn't drop. The price had gone up, the margins improved, and Ritchie definitely could pick and choose his customers. Like most pumps, he had a big sign, saying 'REGULAR CUSTOMERS ONLY'. And everyone paid – or no petrol. And everyone was limited to perhaps a gallon. No exceptions. But Ritchie was now getting paid for every drop that flowed from his pumps.

Even some of the long-standing debtors had to pay off their debts before they could come near Ritchie looking for petrol, as they had debts everywhere else and couldn't get credit. He used to tell me of the return of people who he never expected. They had to come back to Ritchie, as other filling stations were only serving their regulars. Of course, those who hadn't been with Ritchie for months thought that Ritchie might have forgotten about the old debts and some of them pretended to have forgotten about their past dues themselves, but Ritchie didn't forget. Mrs. Porter had it all written down in a notebook, every drop that was owed and by whom.

I was like everyone else. I was afraid that I would suffer from the embargo as well.

But then, just in my hour of need, who was my saving grace – my St. Jude, as my mother would have said? Yes, Ritchie.

Ritchie was my personal Oil Sheikh.

I always say that you always remember a good turn and you never forget a bad one!

And Ritchie remembered the good turns.

Ritchie would let me know approximately when he was getting his petrol from the wholesaler. They were obviously rationed too, but they looked after *their* regular customers too. The deliveries were staggered as well, to prevent queues forming at all hours of the early morning. A delivery could have been midday or midnight. The petrol station owners got very little notice. Maybe a day or so – or even less.

So all through the crisis, I would stop with Ritchie, each evening on the way home to see if he knew when his next delivery would be. If there were a few people about, or a queue, or he wasn't due a delivery that night, Ritchie would call to me, "Sorry, son, no petrol," and wave me away.

But when Ritchie knew his delivery was imminent, he would let me know by simply telling me. If there were people around, he would call to me, "Sorry, son, no petrol," and wave me on – but as he did, he would step a bit closer to the car and give me a wink. That was enough.

I would drive on home and later that night and put four plastic drums, each holding five gallons, neatly into the boot of my car, and I would then drive up to Lifford about 11.30 p.m. and park round the side of Ritchie's house. Now, another car wouldn't be noticed in Ritchie's forecourt anyway. The reason was that Ritchie had several sons and daughters and there were always more than a few cars about. It was a rare night that half a dozen vehicles or more, were not parked willy-nilly outside Ritchie's home.

So as soon as Ritchie's quota arrived by tanker lorry, I was first out of the traps, pulled up beside the pumps and got my twenty gallons of petrol in the drums in the boot – AND a full tank!

There was no shortage of petrol for me, I could have sold the stuff to the Arabs!

As soon as I paid Ritchie, I headed home with my load of petrol. I suppose it was a dangerous enough operation to be at. But I drove very slowly and carefully. I had enough for both me and my father. As soon as I got home, we removed the drums from the boot, took them up to the fir trees at the top of the garden for safety and next morning, we poured the petrol from the drums into a large barrel, which we had hidden deep in the trees. I even had a tap fitted to the barrel, so all we had to do was fill what we needed from the barrel.

Petrol embargo – what petrol embargo?

I had been fair with Ritchie and he certainly returned the favour.

If memory serves me well, the petrol shortage lasted about six months and the embargo was lifted and petrol was plentiful again.

Things slowly returned to normal. Almost.

Shortly afterwards I was transferred from Strabane to Enniskillen and I saw less of Ritchie. However, the clock was ticking for Ritchie – and indeed for thousands of other small independent petrol retailers all over the country. The big multinationals were squeezing the small man and there was always going to be only one winner.

Part Four – Wake Night

Ritchie struggled on until about 1980, but eventually he had to call a halt. Ritchie retired.

He and his wife and family moved into Lifford town to live. It was closer to the shops, etc. When Ritchie did move, that was the last I saw of him. As I have already related at the beginning of this story, I had intended visiting him on several occasions, but to my shame, I never did. Then, about 1985, I heard one day that Ritchie had passed away. Suddenly, it was said. He had been working at home when he was struck down with a heart attack.

When I heard that, I really regretted not having gone to visit him while he was alive.

So I vowed to go and pay my respects at his wake. It was the least I could do. So that night, I got dressed in my best and off I went to Lifford. As I passed the old place where Ritchie's home and petrol pumps were it was now dark, and my mind returned to those days, many years ago, when, in the midst of a nationwide petrol drought, I had all the petrol I needed. The pumps were long gone. Nothing remained to indicate that a filling station had ever existed there. And now Ritchie too was gone. But in my memory, I could see the big Shell sign, brightly lit at night, the pumps, the steady stream of cars, all coming and going and all parked in his forecourt everywhere, and Ritchie, with his wee hat on, racing around.

Now, it was silent and there wasn't a car to be seen. A solitary light could be seen behind a drawn curtain. How life changes!

A few minutes later and I arrived in the Main Street in Lifford. The front door to Ritchie's house was open and as usual, a row of cars lined both sides of the street. Many of Ritchie's family had married and had kids of their own, so Ritchie's house was even more so a hive of activity, especially tonight, now that Ritchie was being waked. It will be a big wake, I thought to myself, as I went round Harte's corner, drove on to the Brock's shop and did a U-turn and came back over Butcher Street, and got parked up in front of Harte's Bar. At least I was facing home, should there be more traffic. Which I had no doubt there would be, as the night progressed and more people arrived to pay their respects.

I got out and walked to the house, stepped in the front door and rapped the inside door. A moment later, a girl opened it. It was one of Ritchie's daughters, I knew that much, but I couldn't remember her name. She looked at me with some puzzlement and eventually she said,

"You're…you're…ah, you're the fella who worked in the bank, aren't you?" She just couldn't remember my name, either.

"Frank McGurk," I said, softly. I could see quite a few people inside.

"Oh, Jesus…aye…Frank McGurk. Frank, come in, come on in!" she said, as she opened the door wider.

I shook her hand and mumbled the well-worn words, "I'm sorry to hear about your dad."

Curiously, she didn't reply. She turned and called, "Mammy, Mammy, come 'ere, come 'ere. Look who's just come in."

Mrs. Porter came over and when saw me, she clasped my hand in her two hands and began to cry. She began shaking her head and just said, "Ah, Frank, Frank, Frank."

After a pause, I leaned down and said,

177

"I'm sorry to hear about Ritchie, Mrs. Porter. I just heard, today. It must have been a terrible shock." I paused for a moment, trying to think of something more to say, as she wept.

So I then said, "Sudden, was it?"

"Aye, very sudden," she said, trying to find a dry corner of her hankie. "He was down the back as usual, footering in the garden and just collapsed. I found him, just lying there in the yard."

"Heart?" I asked.

"Aye, heart attack," she said. And she kept shaking my hand.

"And what age was he?" I asked, trying to slowly lessen her grip, but she was having none of it.

"Just sixty-eight," she said, "just sixty-eight…Ah, Frank, many's the time we talked about you, you were so good to us." she said, shaking her head and drying her tears with a handkerchief. She turned to her daughter. "Margaret, bring Frank a cup of tea. Ah, Frank, you were good to us, so you were. Sure we were just talking about you the other night."

She still didn't slacken the grip on my hand. I didn't know what else to say, but eventually I said, "No, Mrs. Porter. Sure it was yourself and Ritchie who were good to me, when there was no petrol to be had anywhere. And your tea and toast those cold mornings, sure I'll never forget it."

Neither of us spoke for a moment.

After the pause, I said quietly, "You'll miss him terribly, so you will."

She looked up at me quizzically. "Miss him? How do you mean, 'miss him'?"

I mumbled something like, "Well, when the funeral's over and all that. and you're here on your own…"

"Funeral…???" she said very quietly. *"What funeral?"*

Her grip slackened. I felt the room starting to revolve like a scene from Hitchcock's *Vertigo*…

"Ah no, sure he's not dead, thank God," she said, she finally released her grip of my hand and pointed to the ceiling. "He's lying up there in the room. The doctor says he should be okay."

If ever I needed a massive big hole, to swallow me up, it was then. All I could think was *Jesus Christ, get me out of here, quick!*

Mrs. Porter was still talking, but I wasn't listening to her anymore. Her voice was miles away. I tried to speak, but nothing would come out for a moment, then I said something like, "I'm sorry, Mrs. Porter, I heard he had died."

"Ah, no," she repeated. "He's not dead, thanks be to Jesus. Close call, mind you."

Her daughter handed me the cup of tea. Her mother was smiling a little as she said to her, "Frank here thought that your daddy was dead. Somebody told him that."

The daughter didn't know whether to laugh or cry. I was busy trying to explain that I had heard he had died.

"Jesus, I hope not," said her daughter. "At least he wasn't dead the last time I was up the stairs, anyway."

I took two sips of the tea and couldn't wait to get away.

I felt that everyone in the room was staring at me, laughing at me, all of them.

Somebody called, "Mammy," and Mrs. Porter turned to me. "You sit down there, Frank, I'll be back in a minute," nodding at a chair and walking back to the kitchen. She had no sooner turned her back, when I quietly set down the cup, kept my head as low as I could, opened the door, slipped out and closed it ever so quietly behind me, and sprinted away, literally.

I was never as broken in my whole life. I ran down around the corner to my car, unlocked it and pulled open the door, jumped in, started her up, slammed her into first, rounded Harte's corner like a rally driver and drove out of Lifford like the proverbial bat-out-of-hell.

As I passed the old pumps, I put the boot down even further and didn't dare to look in.

I even imagined that Ritchie was in the back seat, laughing, like the way the monster laughs in a scene in one from those horror films. A half laugh, half scream. But I dared not look around – or even glance in the mirror. I got so frightened that I thought for a moment I heard the Banshee!

I never slackened up until I got home, pulled into the yard and switched off the ignition. I sat there in silence and said to myself, "Jesus Christ, what a fool, I must have looked. I'll be the talk of the country."

After I gave myself a few moments to calm down and settle myself, I went into the house. My wife, Audrey, says, "Well, you didn't stay long. Big wake, was it?"

"Aye," says I. "Big wake, my arse – Ritchie isn't even dead!"

When I told her what happened, she burst into a fit of laughing and all I could do after a few minutes was laugh as well.

I always had the intention of going back up to Lifford and sitting down with Ritchie and his wife and having a good laugh about it. But I just couldn't bring myself to call. I just couldn't.

Ritchie never really did get over his heart attack. It knocked him back a good bit and he finally did get to his rest, about three years later.

When I heard – again – my first reaction was to go to his wake. But then I thought, how could I go up to the house again, walk in and shake Mrs. Porter's hand and say,

"I'm sorry to hear about Ritchie, Mrs. Porter, I just heard, today. It must have been a terrible shock. Sudden, was it?"

No, I don't think so, either. All I could imagine was walking in the door and everyone bursting out laughing and pointing at me!

Mrs. Porter, herself, God bless her, died a couple of years ago.

I still pass Ritchie's old place regularly and while there's nothing now to show that it ever was a filling station, I cannot help remembering the old days. The fills of petrol late in the night, the tea and toast in the mornings from Mrs. Porter, while Ritchie made up his lodgement. And his wee hat, I don't think I ever saw him without it.

I suppose at times, when I think back, it *was* a struggle for them.

But not nearly as big a struggle as it was for me, to get away from that house in Lifford, like a bolt of lightning, the night Ritchie Porter 'died'!

The End

Frank McGurk
August 2022